Endorsement from Dr. Thelma Wells, D. D. (Mama T)

In today's world it seems that our hearts are more distracted than ever. Our minds and lives can be overwhelmed when we read the daily news, watch the sights on TV, juggle our schedules, or even interact with social media. But I'm excited to engage you in one of the most powerful and refreshing devotionals of this season! It is one that can help ease your mind, settle your spirit, and spread the joy of the Lord into your soul. Release into your spirit, the calm assurance of the Lord's peace as you relax from a distracted heart with Peg Arnold!

DEVOTIONS FOR THE

Distracted Heart

DEVOTIONS FOR THE
Distracted Heart

PEG ARNOLD
Chicken Soup for the Soul Contributing Author

wonder *of* women

Peg Arnold © 2019
Email: pegarnoldwow@gmail.com
Website: www.pegarnold.org
Blog: https://pegarnold.wordpress.com/

All rights reserved. No part of this publication may be reproduced, stored in a retrieval system, or transmitted in any form or by any means—electronic, mechanical, photocopy, recording, or any other without the prior permission of the author.

ISBN-13: 978-1-7327699-2-2

Library of Congress Control Number: 2019903511

Unless otherwise noted, all scripture is taken from THE HOLY BIBLE, NEW INTERNATIONAL VERSION®, NIV® Copyright © 1973, 1978, 1984, 2011 by Biblica, Inc.® Used by permission. All rights reserved worldwide.
"Scripture from *The Message*. Copyright © 1993, 1994, 1995, 1996, 2000, 2001, 2002. Used by permission of NavPress Publishing Group."
Holy Bible, New Living Translation (NLT), copyright © 1996, 2004, 2015 by Tyndale House Foundation. Used by permission of Tyndale House Publishers, Inc.,
The Living Bible copyright © 1971 by Tyndale House Foundation. Used by permission of Tyndale House Publishers Inc., Carol Stream, Illinois 60188. All rights reserved. The Living Bible, TLB, and the The Living Bible logo are registered trademarks of Tyndale House Publishers. Carol Stream, Illinois 60188. All rights reserved.

Printed in the United States of America

Cover Designer & Typesetter: Michelle Kenny, Windsor, CO

This book is a celebration of time, prayer, and support from family and friends who have walked through many of these experiences with me. I especially appreciate those who have supported me with the editing, endorsement, and loving encouragement.

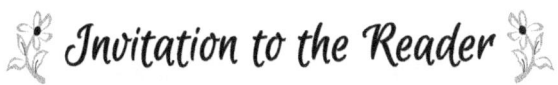

Invitation to the Reader

Each devotion focuses on common distractions that often detour our day. Some are the result of life's typical interruptions while others can be more unusual. The reflections are designed to reveal God's presence and His support in our distractions. Whether you read these daily or weekly, it is my prayer that you will sense His peace and grow in your relationship with Christ.

How to use this devotional:

1. These messages are organized into 8 weeks.
2. Each entry has scripture, devotion, and a prayer.
3. You may read them in any order. There is a box next to each entry in the Table of Contents to check as you complete it.
4. A companion journal, *Devotions for the Distracted Heart —Journal,* is available.

Table of Contents

Invitation to the Reader ix

Week 1

- ❏ Distraction of Decisions 2
- ❏ Distraction of Dilemmas 5
- ❏ Distraction of Digital Devices 8
- ❏ Distraction of the Desert 12
- ❏ Distraction of Dogs 16

Week 2

- ❏ Distraction of Details 22
- ❏ Distraction of Deception 25
- ❏ Distraction of Drains 30
- ❏ Distraction of Disability 34
- ❏ Distraction of Devastation 38

Week 3

- ☐ Distraction of DIY 44
- ☐ Distraction of Darkness 48
- ☐ Distraction of Discipline 51
- ☐ Distraction of Directions 54
- ☐ Distraction of Dementia 58

Week 4

- ☐ Distraction of Dialogue 64
- ☐ Distraction of Discontent 68
- ☐ Distraction of Dependence 72
- ☐ Distraction of Denali 76
- ☐ Distraction of Despair 79

Week 5

- ☐ Distraction of Diets 84
- ☐ Distraction of Deterioration 87
- ☐ Distraction of Death 90
- ☐ Distraction of Ducks 94
- ☐ Distraction of Displacement 98

Table of Contents

Week 6

- ❏ Distraction of Detox 104
- ❏ Distraction of Delayed Departures 108
- ❏ Distraction of Diapers 111
- ❏ Distraction of Delayed Responses 114
- ❏ Distraction of Denim 118

Week 7

- ❏ Distraction of Disappointment 124
- ❏ Distraction of Decluttering 128
- ❏ Distraction of Diamonds 132
- ❏ Distraction of Departures from the Familiar 135
- ❏ Distraction of Dessert 138

Week 8

- ❏ Distraction of Doors 144
- ❏ Distraction of Departures 147
- ❏ Distraction of Detours 150
- ❏ Distraction of Doubt 153
- ❏ Distraction of Dislocation 156

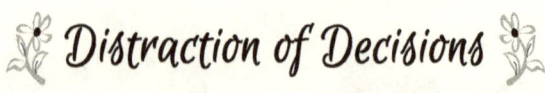 Distraction of Decisions

> *I will praise the Lord, who counsels me; even at night my heart instructs me. I keep my eyes always on the Lord. With Him at my right hand, I will not be shaken.*
> —Psalm 16:7–8

Decisions, decisions! From the time we wake up to the moment we fall asleep we are making choices. What to wear and eat, when to wake or sleep, what to say, who to call or text, where to go, what to watch – the list is endless. In addition, we choose how we care for our children, parents, spouses, friends, and others. It can be overwhelming!

Some decisions are carefully designed by weighing the pros and cons, researching options, or investigating alternatives. Other decisions are more spontaneous. Sometimes we seek counsel from experts or friends. Depending on the importance of the decision, the process can consume our thoughts, exhaust our energies, and debilitate our actions.

I'm embarrassed to admit that in my graduate program, I studied many decision-making structures equipping me with the knowledge and resources for making wise choices. In spite of these tools and my internal desire to succeed, unexpected interferences easily distract me and derail my motivation in routine decisions causing procrastination. The result can be a poor decision or a disappointing outcome. In these cases, I have no one to blame but myself for my own poor judgment. Sometimes the results of my hasty decisions impact the lives of others. When this happens, I become stressed and beat myself up with negative messages. In fact, I lose sleep, replaying the situation over and over in my head, reminding me of my need to seek forgiveness and God's reassurance. Psalm 16:7–8 affirms that if I listen, the Lord will provide instruction and counsel in those restless nights. *I will praise the Lord, who counsels me; even at night my heart instructs me. I keep my eyes always on the Lord. With Him at my right hand, I will not be shaken.*

Through scripture and prayers, the Lord reassures me that I am still loved and valuable. In spite of my poor decisions, worry, or lack of judgment, He remains the constant source of strength, wisdom, and courage. Focusing on Christ helps me to accept His forgiveness as well as to forgive myself for poor choices. This enables me to learn from each situation, pressing on to the next opportunity ahead. ♥

Devotions for the Distracted Heart

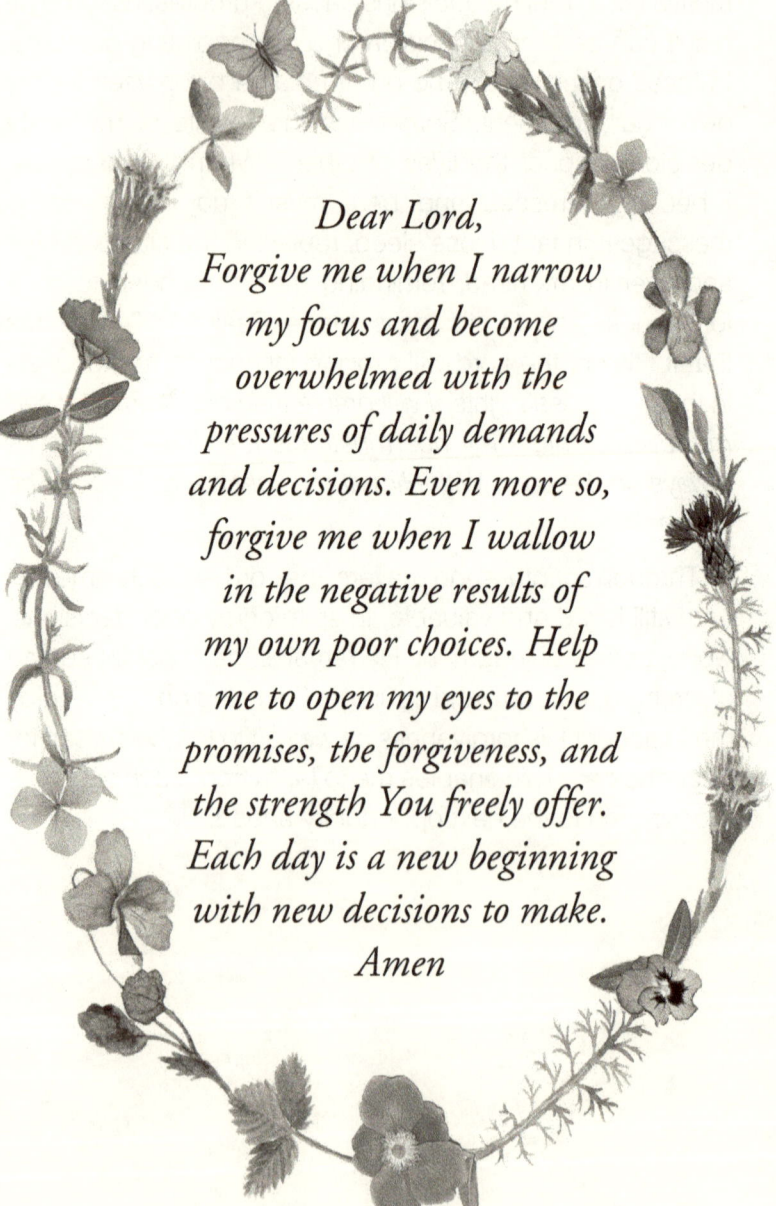

*Dear Lord,
Forgive me when I narrow my focus and become overwhelmed with the pressures of daily demands and decisions. Even more so, forgive me when I wallow in the negative results of my own poor choices. Help me to open my eyes to the promises, the forgiveness, and the strength You freely offer. Each day is a new beginning with new decisions to make.
Amen*

Distraction of Dilemmas

> "Which of these three do you think was a neighbor to the man who fell into the hands of robbers?" The expert in the law replied, "The one who had mercy on him." Jesus told him, "Go and do likewise."
> —Luke 10:36–37

After a hectic morning of running errands with a kindergartner and a toddler, I just wanted to get home, drop my daughter off at school, and put my son down for a nap! In fact, I was ready for a nap, too! Racing up the familiar road, I saw the lights of a police cruiser with 2 cars pulled over to the side. Wanting to pass by this obstruction and get home, I recognized a dear friend and her child standing at the side of the road talking with the policeman. With a fussy toddler and a daughter to drop off at school, I felt a sense of helplessness and insatiable guilt as I drove by without stopping. The silhouettes of my friend and her daughter watching me drive away haunted me the rest of the way home.

I struggled with the dilemma of stopping to help or getting my daughter to school on time and justified my decision by praying for her out loud with my children listening. Concerned and determined to help, I resolved to return to the accident scene after I dropped my daughter off at school. Wrong decision! By the time I arrived at the bend in the road, the accident was cleaned up and no one was left to help or comfort.

Nearly thirty years later, I still struggle with that decision. I will never forget the feeling in the pit of my stomach when I returned to that empty shoulder. Let alone, the look of hurt when I attempted to justify my decisions the next time I saw my friend and her daughter. My plea for forgiveness seemed empty as I tried to defend my lack of compassion with;

"The kids were fussy and I saw that you had help already."

"I went back, I really did, but you weren't there, I was praying for you the whole time."

By the look on her face, it was clear that my pleas for forgiveness didn't cover the pain caused by the overshadowing sense of abandonment.

I internally chastised myself and was continually haunted with the images of the crumpled fender and forlorn silhouettes. Could I have at least just stopped to offer a hug? Yes. Could I have stopped and taken her daughter with me? Yes. That day, I was faced with an immediate dilemma and, I confess, I did not make the right choice.

We face dilemmas every day. Sometimes there isn't enough time to weigh all the pros and cons before making a decision. I learned an important lesson from this experience. First, I tend to schedule myself tightly, leaving

Distraction of Dilemmas

no margin for error, detours, or for attending to the needs of others. Second, in the midst of an over-packed schedule, it is not always convenient to do what Jesus would do.

The other part of this dilemma was the priority I modeled to my daughter. Yes, praying for someone in need is important, but I missed the opportunity to demonstrate Christ's compassion in action. Instead I felt I demonstrated that her school schedule was more important than helping someone.

I felt as if I was the Levite in the story of the Good Samaritan, totally self-absorbed in my obligations and insensitive to the needs of someone else. My friend has since gone to be with the Lord. I know that she eventually forgave me for the decision I made that hectic morning. But have I forgiven myself? Have I changed my ways and stopped scheduling my days so tightly? Do I live on a narrow track that doesn't allow detours to stop and demonstrate Christ's compassion? What dilemmas might you face today? ♥

Dear Lord, Help me as I go through this day to see where I can be Your hands and feet in the world. When faced with dilemmas, grant me wisdom to choose relationships over tasks and obligations. For I know that when I reach out to the least of these, I have reached out to You. Amen

Distraction of Digital Devices

> *Do not conform to the pattern of this world, but be transformed by the renewing of your mind. Then you will be able to test and approve what God's will is—his good, pleasing and perfect will.* —Romans 12:2

It's a wild, wonderful world filled with gadgets and gizmos to make our lives easier. Our smartphones give us immediate access to information anytime, anywhere (as long as there is a signal available). We can even program unique sounds: bells, barks, chirps, music, and/or pings to make sure we receive a notification for every email, text, score, post, and more. By receiving these alerts, we are assured of staying up to date with all our online connections. I've heard this referred to as the phenomena of *Fear of Missing Out,* better known as FOMO. This is the need to immediately know when anything occurs so that one can live informed and be able to respond. We see this everywhere we go. People of all ages have their heads buried in their digital devices, living more life through the cyber world than in person. I have to admit, I can be guilty of this, too.

Before we had cell phones, I remember a retreat discussion about the urgency of answering our "land

Distraction of Digital Devices

line" phone or even the doorbell. We debated whether we should allow the phone call to be a priority that interrupted all current interactions. Then the urgency of answering a phone call subsided with the introduction of the answering machine and caller ID. Yet now, have we allowed the notifications on our digital devices to have the same control in our lives?

True confession – when I got my first smart phone, I thought it was great to know when a new picture was posted, a text or email came in, or even be reminded that I hadn't read my devotion yet for the day. However, these notifications started disrupting my life while I was driving, at dinner with a friend or family, and even when I was sleeping! Then I realized the truth. I was allowing these notifications to take priority in my day. I needed to ask myself these questions. Was every message important enough to check immediately? Did I need to know each time a new post was added to a conversation queue? I began to realize I had swallowed the Kool-Aid of the FOMO syndrome, and my cyber-world was receiving more of my attention than my real world. I immediately began to remove the notifications from almost every app on my phone.

Oh, don't get me wrong. I think there are many wonderful aspects of my digital device that keep my life organized and more efficient. I truly appreciate the reminders for calendar events, I keep track of my calories, monitor my exercise, and have access to all types of devotions including reading through the Bible. I use the notifications to alert me of a text or a call. However, I confess that even without the extra digital notification disruptions, I can still get lost in

Devotions for the Distracted Heart

my phone. It may be reading and communicating with others on text, email, or social networks, checking out all the possibilities while planning a vacation, searching a new recipe, or even playing a game with a friend. I need to ask myself: is my digital device enhancing my relationships or distracting from my relationships, both at home and with God?

There is a quote from the movie, *The Devil Wears Prada,* when the main character is arguing with her boyfriend. In the middle of a tearful exchange, the ringing of her cell phone disrupts their serious conversation. Instead of ignoring the ring, she immediately takes the call. Her upset boyfriend shakes his head, begins to leave, and says "The person whose calls you always take? That's the relationship you're in" (The Devil Wears Prada, 2006).

So I ask myself these questions:

- Concerning the distraction of digital disruptions, what relationships am I valuing?
- Am I being a good steward of my time?
- If I were to graph out my time, would it reflect my desired priorities?

I have heard of people going on digital fasts. I'm not sure I need to do this yet, but being intentional and disciplined about the use of my digital device might be a way to begin. Am I the only one? How about you?

Distraction of Digital Devices

*Dear Lord,
With so much going on,
help me to focus on the
priorities and the blessings You
have given me. This world is filled
with many challenges and many
joys. Guide my decisions and
time as I work towards putting
away the "things of this world".
Help me to use these man-made
conveniences to enhance my relationships,
my personal growth, and my witness
for You. It is my desire to not
conform to the things of this
world, but be transformed by
renewing my mind in You.
Amen*

Distraction of the Desert

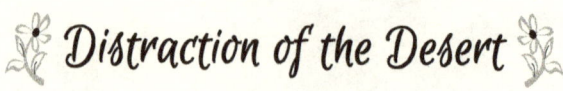

> *My flesh and my heart may fail, but God is the strength of my heart and my portion forever*
> —Psalm 73:26

I love the beach! I grew up visiting the shores of Lake Michigan and never experienced an ocean surf until I travelled to Florida at the age of fourteen. I was amazed at the similarity of the two. They are both expanses of water that continue into the horizon. I loved the bigger waves of the ocean and was fascinated by the effects of the tide. But the part of the ocean I witnessed did not have the same expanse of sand dunes as are around Lake Michigan. These dunes are the closest I have come to experiencing a desert.

When I was a teenager, my friends and I would often take day trips to Silver Lake Dunes. These were miles of sand dunes that began at Silver Lake and connected to the shores of Lake Michigan. We would spend the day hiking across the sandy hills to swim in the lake, and then hike back to the car. I remember the first time I took this journey. It was recommended to wear shoes; I wore flip flops. It was recommended to wear sunscreen and a shirt for added

Distraction of the Desert

protection; I wore coconut oil and a bikini top. It was also recommended to carry water; I took just a towel. Needless to say, I was quite unprepared for the two mile hike over the scorching, hot dunes.

At first we were all filled with excitement for the day. None of us had any idea of the challenges we would face on the hike to the lake. We started walking, laughing, running up the dunes, and rolling down the dunes. We weaved our way through the sea grasses on the hills and in the valleys. It was not long before we started getting hot and tired. I recall reaching the top of one hill, my feet blistered from the burning sand, throat parched from the lack of water, and shoulders burned by the scorching sun. As I turned to look at the view, I was surrounded by 360 degrees of ribbons of sand covered hills. Is this what it's like to be lost in a desert, to be over heated, parched, and exhausted?

Is this similar to what the Israelites felt as they gathered all their belongings and followed Moses into the desert to escape Pharaoh's persecution of slavery? They began the trip with excitement and anticipation of a new life and new opportunities to live independent lives. They hiked for days in the desert, but that excitement wore off as they became hungry and tired of traveling. They even became doubtful of God's promises and challenged Moses, *"What have you done by bringing us out of Egypt?"* Moses responded with a Word from the Lord, *"Do not be afraid. Stand firm and you will see the deliverance the LORD will bring you today. . . The LORD will fight for you; you need only to be still,"* Exodus 14:13a, 14.

The desert is the place we find ourselves when we are challenged by distressing situations, times of abandonment, losses, or difficult relationships. When we experience these trials, we can be overwhelmed by exhaustion, confusion, despair, loneliness, or doubt. We try to look ahead to the horizon of hope, but we are surrounded by 360 degrees of unchanging landscape. If we had a choice, we would not enter these desert times. But God never promises us lives of ease, without pain and challenges. He does, however, promise He will never leave us or forsake us. For the Israelites, He brought a pillar of cloud to protect them from the Egyptians and with Moses' leadership the Lord led them safely through the Red Sea.

What desert are you wandering in today? The God of the Israelites is the same God of today. He is protecting you and going before you through the dark waters, even though you cannot see Him. Remember *For this God is our God for ever and ever; he will be our guide even to the end,* Psalm 48:14.

Distraction of the Desert

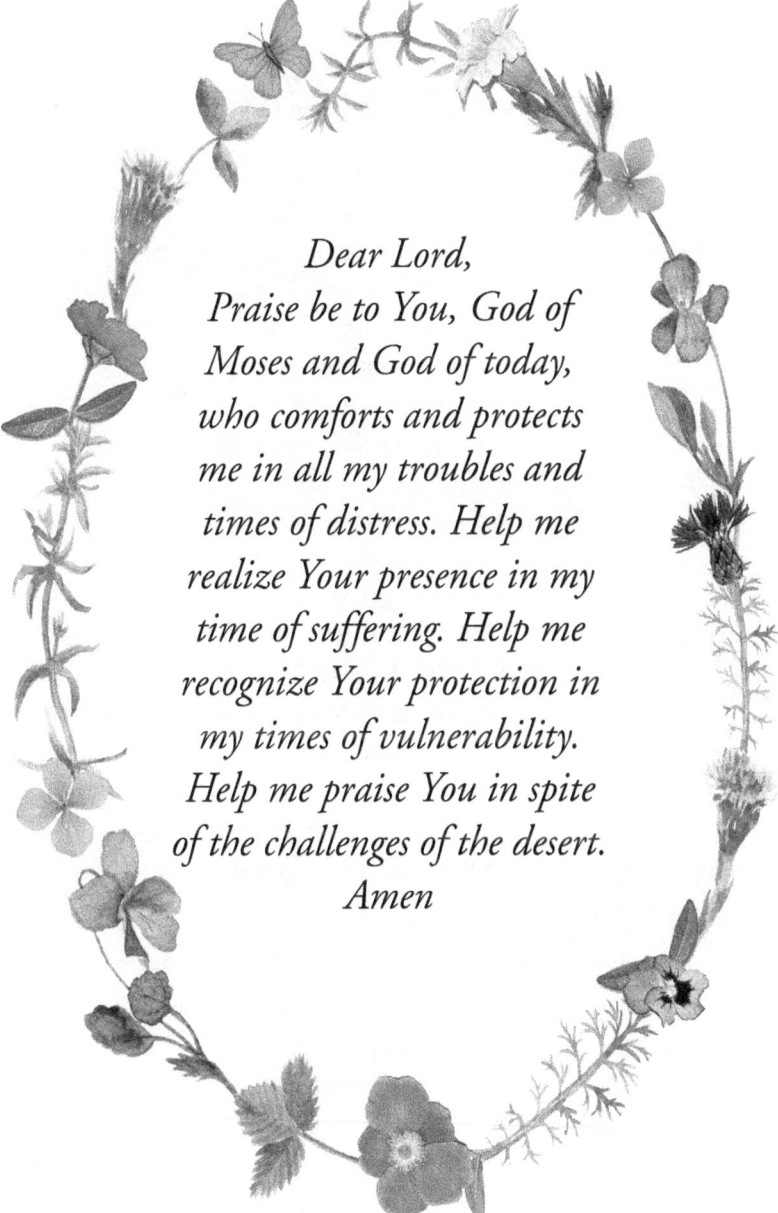

*Dear Lord,
Praise be to You, God of
Moses and God of today,
who comforts and protects
me in all my troubles and
times of distress. Help me
realize Your presence in my
time of suffering. Help me
recognize Your protection in
my times of vulnerability.
Help me praise You in spite
of the challenges of the desert.
Amen*

❦ Distraction of Dogs ❦

> *For I am convinced that nothing can ever separate us from his love. Death can't, and life can't. The angels won't, and all the powers of hell itself cannot keep God's love away. Our fears for today, our worries about tomorrow, or where we are—high above the sky, or in the deepest ocean—nothing will ever be able to separate us from the love of God demonstrated by our Lord Jesus Christ when he died for us.* —Romans 8:38–39 TLB

J married a dog lover. He grew up with a very special dog and always wanted us to have one after we got married. In fact, before we even talked about it, he brought me the gift of two puppies, hoping I would fall in love with the little fur balls. Well, I have to admit, they were adorable. However, playing with other people's puppies is completely different from owning them and being responsible for their needs from day to day.

Not being a dog lover, I had very little patience for the messes and accidents that come with having puppies. I grew impatient when they whined at night, and I often mourned the casualties of chewed shoes and scratched furniture. Every time we left the house, we returned to a floor covered with dirt and shredded leaves from a favorite plant, tufts of cotton from disassembled pillows, or debris from trash cans. Even when we tried to contain the puppies in a small room with all vulnerable items removed, they actually chewed the corners of the walls and door! Needless to say, it was a very challenging time in our marriage. It took the loss of a fourth pair of shoes and a golf club grip before my husband agreed to give both dogs away to loving homes.

Now, compare this experience to the puppy we got twelve years later. We researched dogs, included the kids in our decision process, and went together as a family to get our first dog. The night Mysti came into our home, she whined and cried keeping everyone awake. She had similar accidents, chewed shoes and ruined furniture. She brought all the extra dirt into the house that the other dogs did, but my heart was in a different place with Mysti. I loved having her in our family and watching the kid's excitement as they played and cuddled with her.

I have since watched each of my children bring dogs into their homes. They care for them and coddle them as they do their own children. They embrace the responsibilities and challenges of dog ownership with patience. In turn, these dogs are an integral part of their lives, showering them with slobbery kisses and entertaining them with furry antics. I am amazed as I watch my son sacrificially rise early in the morning and venture into the cold to take their new puppy outside.

I think back to the way I treated those first puppies in my home. I did not even want them. I thought of them as an inconvenience, an annoyance, a frustration in my life. My love for them was completely conditional and offered only when they were cute and cooperative. What if God treated

Devotions for the Distracted Heart

us like that? What if His love was conditional and dependent on our daily faithfulness to Him? I don't know about you, but I would never measure up. I could never earn the love of Jesus by the things I do. Unlike the dogs, I do not tear up belongings in my house, but I misuse and squander many of the gifts God gives me. I clutter my mind with negative thoughts, worry, and frustration. I make promises of commitment to God only to fail following through the next day. I waste the gift of time with activities that distract me from the knowledge of His presence. Yet no matter what I do, God is patient with me. His word constantly reminds me that He is there and will never forsake me even when I feel distant and lost. There is nothing that can separate me from His love. ♥

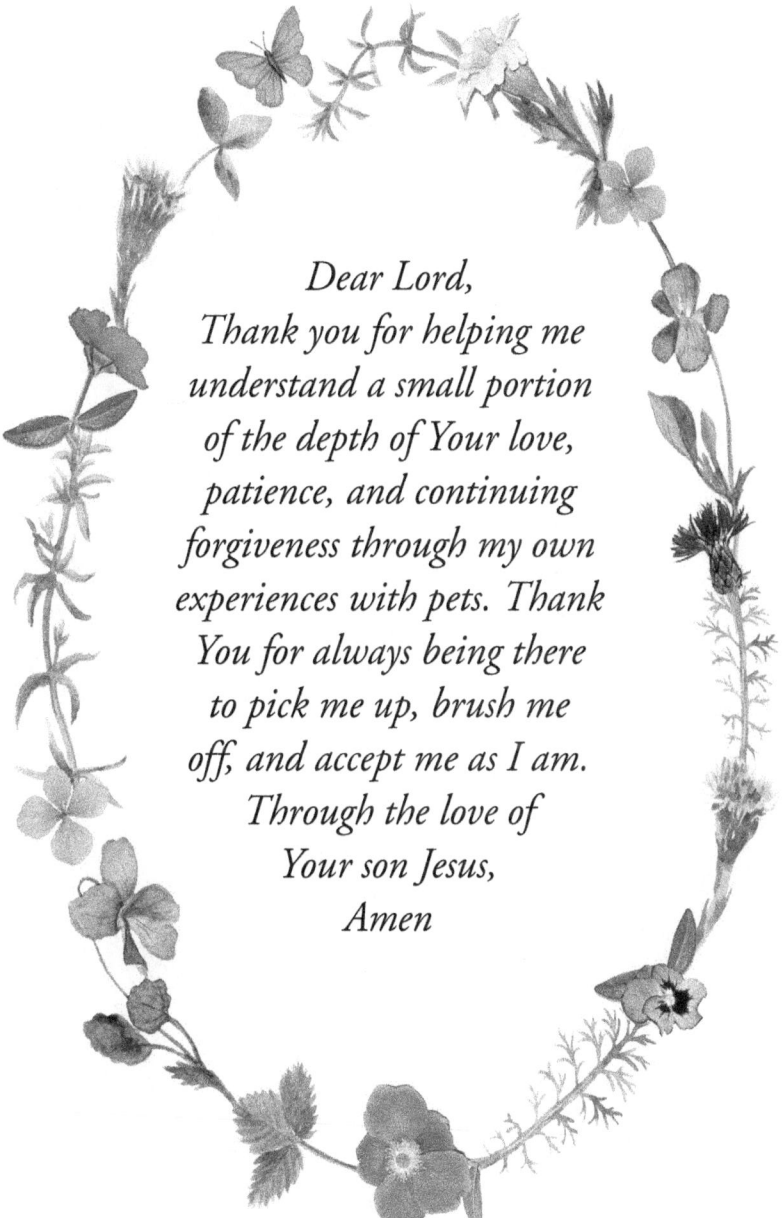

*Dear Lord,
Thank you for helping me understand a small portion of the depth of Your love, patience, and continuing forgiveness through my own experiences with pets. Thank You for always being there to pick me up, brush me off, and accept me as I am. Through the love of Your son Jesus,
Amen*

Distraction of Details

> *You have looked deep into my heart,
> Lord, and you know all about me.*
> —Psalm 139:1

I am a list person. I have lists for everything: work and home projects, weekly chores, groceries, recipes to try, cards to send, and more. These lists can be found everywhere: in my purse and desk, on the refrigerator, and even next to my bed (this is the list I make when I can't sleep at night because of all the details swimming in my head). My new found friend is the reminder list on my smartphone. I put items on that app and even schedule notifications to increase my accountability to the time sensitive items.

Why do I encumber myself with these lists? I think they provide me security, because they help me remember important tasks, and I feel a sense of accomplishment when I can cross off items. Sometimes I measure my personal value by the accomplishment of these daily tasks. There is an actual adrenalin rush in disposing of a completed list!

However, they can produce unnecessary stress or guilt when I don't complete all of them. In fact, I have difficulty forgiving myself when I do not meet personal deadlines

Distraction of Details

and call myself names: list loser, detail dumper, finish failure. Feeling defeated, I reorganize the same items on newly constructed lists hoping for future success.

I don't believe God wants me to live this way – overwhelmed with unrealistic details and deadlines and measuring my worth by the number of tasks I complete. I think He sees my lists as distracting clutter, blinding me from the plans He has for me. I am so busy trying to complete my plans, I am missing His blessings.

David wrote about how God knows about the most intimate details of our lives; *You have looked deep into my heart, Lord, and you know all about me,* Psalm 139:1. You see, God knows our lists and desires, what we will accomplish and what things will be left undone. He even knows when we will be so distracted by our tasks and details that we leave Him out. If we take everything to Him, He will be there to reassure us. He is with us and will help us. It is when we try to accomplish our goals alone that we can either become discouraged by our failure to complete the tasks, or possibly arrogant by the success of our own achievements.

This psalm goes on to say; *You know when I am resting or when I am working and from heaven you discover my thoughts. You notice everything I do and everywhere I go. Before I even speak a word, you know what I will say,* Psalm 139:2–4. If this were written today it might say; *Lord, You know what I will text, the lists I will make, the details that will distract me, the reminders I will ignore, and the ones I will heed,* Peg Arnold 2019.

Devotions for the Distracted Heart

How wonderful that we have a God who cares about the details of our lives. He knows when we will fail and succeed, yet He still patiently waits for us. *I can't understand all of this! Such wonderful knowledge is far above me,* Psalm 139:6. ♥

Dear Lord, You have searched me and know the desires of my heart. You know my comings and goings, joys and sorrows, successes and failures. Even before I was born, You knew each moment of my day. Your thoughts are far beyond my own meager understanding. Thank You for the patience You show me each day when I distract myself with details and lists. Forgive me when I value my worth by the tasks I complete rather than the relationships I build. Thank You for being a God of details and eager to help me find my value in Your dreams for me. Amen

 Distraction of Deception

> *If we claim to be without sin, we deceive ourselves and the truth is not in us. If we confess our sins, he is faithful and just and will forgive us our sins and purify us from all unrighteousness.* —James 1:9

I remember when my son was eight years old. He was due home from school when my neighbor called. She had just received a message from a very upset woman who told her that both of our sons were throwing things at passing cars, and her car had been hit. Needless to say, we were not proud of these actions and discussed what we were going to do with the boys. When my son arrived home, I asked him what his day was like and how the walk home went. He replied, "Fine."

"Did anyone stop their car to talk with you on the way home?"

To this he answered, "No," and quickly retreated into the bathroom. While he was in the bathroom, I could hear him talking to himself. "How did she know? How did she know?"

Then he answered himself in a changed voice, "She knew by the guilty look on your face!"

Listening to this was quite entertaining, however, I still needed to follow through with consequences for the poor choice and the deception.

How do we react when we first realize that a child has lied to us? Are we caught in a dilemma between consequences and teachable moments? Do we choose one response or a combination of both?

Whether we realize it or not, we live in a world where deception is acceptable. It is woven into our lives and permeates our society even when we try to avoid it. Media itself is filled with less than truthful information with its reality shows, newscast spins, or commercials touting inflated promises.

Think about it. No one likes to be deceived. In fact, most of us strive to be honest and trustworthy. Honesty is a virtue we teach our children. As parents, teachers, models, and mentors, we take great effort to encourage our children to tell the truth in all things, even if they think they will get in trouble. We explain to them that it is better to get in trouble for being truthful than to tell a lie that delays the consequence.

How did God handle deception? There are many examples in the Bible. The very first one is Adam and Eve. God came strolling in the garden and could not find them. He discovered they were hiding because they had eaten the fruit of the forbidden tree of truth. Do you remember their consequences? They were removed from the garden of paradise and placed in a world where Adam had to work for their food, shelter, and clothing. In addition, Eve was given the sentence of pain in childbirth. We still experience the consequences of their actions today. You see, deception and disobedience were the original sins.

There are other examples of deception in the Bible. Jacob made soup and dressed in the skin of animals to deceive his father Isaac in giving him the blessing due to his older brother, Esau. In this case, Jacob who deceived his father, achieved his goal with what appears to be very little consequence for his sin. But if you follow his life, he became the victim of many deceptions. For instance, when he wanted to marry Laban's daughter, Rachel, Jacob was requested to work for five years and then deceived at the altar when Leah was substituted as the bride. Later, his sons sold their brother Joseph into slavery then deceived their father by telling him that Joseph was killed by a wild animal. There are a multitude of other examples in the Bible and each situation of deception results in life changing consequences.

Sir Walter Scott penned the words, "Oh what a tangled web we weave, when first we practice to deceive!" If we realize that deception is a sin that has negative consequences, why do we fall prey to it? I think there are several reasons.

First, there are times when the falsehood delays an uncomfortable truth. We fool ourselves by the assurance that eventually the truthful details will be shared. Second, there are times we might choose to deceive because honesty would be more hurtful to our friend or family. In this case, we convince ourselves that the deception is a humanitarian or compassionate choice. Third, we might deceive because it avoids an immediate conflict.

Finally, we can deceive by omission. This form of deception is dangerous because we don't recognize it as evil and tend to think we are above reproach.

God's Word tells us; *Therefore each of you must put off falsehood and speak truthfully to your neighbor, for we are all members of one body,* Ephesians 4:25.

How do you approach God when you have been deceitful? I believe that He knows all of our sin before we even admit it to ourselves. Just like with the situation with my son, I knew the truth before he told me, and when he denied it I needed to address that act of dishonesty.

When we recognize deception has crept into our own thoughts, words, or actions, we are instructed to seek forgiveness. *If we confess our sins, he is faithful and just and will forgive us our sins and purify us from all unrighteousness,* 1 John 1:9. We have a loving God who is there with His arms open and ready to forgive.

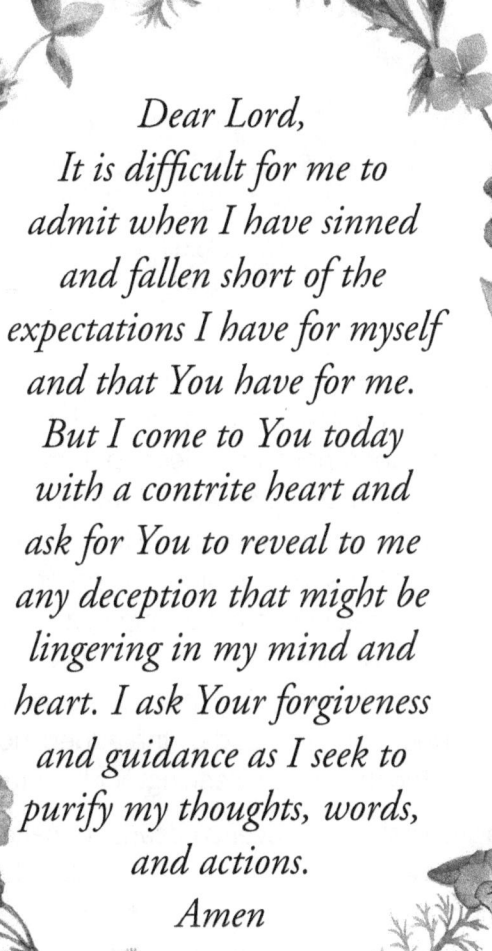

*Dear Lord,
It is difficult for me to admit when I have sinned and fallen short of the expectations I have for myself and that You have for me. But I come to You today with a contrite heart and ask for You to reveal to me any deception that might be lingering in my mind and heart. I ask Your forgiveness and guidance as I seek to purify my thoughts, words, and actions.
Amen*

Distraction of Drains

> *For God did not call us to be impure,*
> *but to live a holy life.*
> —1 Thessalonians 4:7

Clogged drains, what a distraction! I am often not aware when a drain is clogged until it's too late. The inconvenience of repairs and cleanup it creates becomes a "drain" on my emotions as well as my time. For example, when I begin my laundry routine, I try to remember to double check the laundry sink to make sure no objects are in it, as my washing machine empties into that sink. "Try" is the key word! Stepping into a massive puddle when returning to rotate clothes instantly "washes" away my joy. Thus my mood is further compromised by the added inconvenience of mopping the floors and cleaning out the drain.

Clogged drains are never pleasant no matter where you may encounter them. Just this past weekend, as I walked into a public restroom to wash my hands I heard a voice saying, "you might want to use another sink." I turned around to see a maintenance woman with a plunger in her hand. The sink to which she was referring appeared just fine, but when she vigorously plunged the drain, brown water filled with debris bubbled up into the pristine white basin. This is typical with clogged drains. The sink appears to be fine but the drain harbors hidden filth and debris that stealthily accumulates until it obstructs anything else from passing through.

Sometimes I can be like that clogged drain, allowing debilitating debris to build inside and go unchecked in my life, eventually blocking my connection to the Holy Spirit. What could that debris be? It could consist of selfish attitudes, self-pity, unforgiveness, procrastination, pride, unworthiness, or control. Yes, I am vulnerable to them all. Unrecognized, any one of these attitudes has the ability to accumulate and fester inside, obstructing the fruits of the Holy Spirit.

Sometimes I am aware of these negative attitudes inside my spirit and am not ready or willing to address them. These are the times I attempt to create a façade of peace and righteousness so that others cannot see the weaknesses that I harbor. When I do this, I am no better than the Pharisees whom Christ chastised. They worked very hard to appear pure on the outside, yet were filled with corrupt and deceitful attitudes. *Woe to you, teachers of the law and Pharisees you hypocrites! You are like whitewashed tombs, which look beautiful on the outside but on the inside are full of the bones of the dead and everything unclean,* Matthew 23:27.

With God's help and support of trusted friends, I want to begin the process of identifying my own debilitating attitudes and scraping away any barriers of debris inside

Devotions for the Distracted Heart

my spirit. *For God did not call us to be impure, but to live a holy life.* The Message translates this very clearly: *God hasn't invited us into a disorderly, unkempt life but into something holy and beautiful—as beautiful on the inside as the outside.* 1 Thessalonians 4:7. The only way for me to begin this process is to start each day, spending time at the feet of Jesus and laying His word on my heart. This is the beginning of clearing out the debris and allowing the beauty of Christ on the inside to emulate that same beauty on the outside. ♥

> *"Unrecognized, negative attitudes have the ability to accumulate and fester inside, obstructing the fruits of the Holy Spirit."* —Peg Arnold

Dear Lord,
Thank You for loving me and being patient with me. Create in me a pure heart and put a new and right spirit within me. Help me identify the attitudes that are barriers to hearing Your voice and receiving Your word. I desire to be Your vessel, pure inside and outside. Give me the energy to clean out the negative attitudes of my spirit, so that Your love can flow freely through me, and You can use me to be a light to others.
Amen

Distraction of Disability

> *As you learn more and more how God works, you will learn how to do your work. We pray that you'll have the strength to stick it out over the long haul—not the grim strength of gritting your teeth but the glory-strength God gives. It is strength that endures the unendurable and spills over into joy, thanking the Father who makes us strong enough to take part in everything bright and beautiful that he has for us.*
> —Colossians 1:11–12 The Message

Gliding along atop of the smooth water on two skis, I had found my happy place. It had been three years since I had waterskied. I was excited that my stamina held up, and I did not fall. Not realizing how fatigued I was, I thought I'd try again. Long story short, I didn't even make it out of the water when my left ski took an unexpected turn, and I felt a "pop."

I knew something was wrong, but did not realize the magnitude of my injury until I was sitting in the doctor's office hearing words like trauma, fracture, and surgery. Even then, I figured 4-6 weeks of healing and I would be back in the water, but when the nurse handed my husband the 4 month handicapped parking pass, I began to comprehend the impact this would have on my active routine. After surgery, I came home from the hospital bandaged from thigh to ankle. The doctor gave strict instructions, "No weight should be put on the left leg for 6 weeks!"

I'd never had such a severe injury before, so at first I expected to participate in all my commitments. However, being in a wheel chair presented many limitations, and even with pain killers I couldn't ride in a car for two weeks. The mobility restrictions required dependence on my husband for help with every single task, and that was humbling as well as frustrating.

In my inactivity, I succumbed to self-pity. A friend who had experienced a recent injury shared that he felt a loss of identity since he was unable to do the same things he was able to do before the injury. There had to be a purpose in this experience. What was God trying to teach me? Did I place my identity on the activities I was involved in, or was there greater depth to who I am?

Visitors started coming by to wish me well with cards, meals, and flowers. They all shared how they were praying for me. I received numerous phone calls from friends who were concerned with my adjustment to such a stationary life. Many encouraged me to look for the sweetness in this time of restriction. Wouldn't you know it, one of my devotions right before the injury was based on Psalm 46:10; *Be still and know that I am God.* God did not want me to wallow in self-pity, but turn to Him in this time of confinement. He revealed that my situation was very temporary. There are many who live full and rich lives with permanent disabilities far more limiting than mine!

Devotions for the Distracted Heart

It reminded me of the many times I heard Joni Earickson Tada speak. For those who might not know her, she had a diving accident as a teen. A severe spinal cord injury confined her to a wheelchair, leaving her dependent on help for every task as a quadriplegic. In her ministry, she shares how she struggled with her obstacles and permanent limitations. She freely talks about her depression, anger, desire for death, isolation, and more. It was only through an encounter with a friend who introduced her to the Living Lord and the fact that *the Lord had a plan to prosper not to harm her. A plan to give her a hope and a future,* Jeremiah 29:11. She recalls how her chair once represented alienation and confinement. But through the grace of God, the chair now would represent independence, freedom, and mobility. Today, Joni is a well-known artist, gifted vocalist, radio host, author of numerous books, as well as an advocate for disabled persons.

I think each of us deals with a disability of some sort. It may be physical, spiritual, or even self-limiting beliefs. God does not want us to give in or focus on the things we can't do, but instead concentrate on what we can do. He has gifted each of us with abilities, insights, skills, and talents. This does not discount the suffering that we may experience when we are disabled; it only means that God has a purpose for all of us regardless of difficulty or disease.

Colossians says as we learn more about how God works, we can learn how, and what we can do in the midst of the circumstances. We need God's strength to make it through challenges. *It is strength that endures the unendurable and spills over into joy, thanking the Father who makes us strong enough to take part in everything bright and beautiful that He has for us,* Colossians 1:12 (The Message).

Do you have anything that robs you of joy, ambition, or the ability to seek goals? A disability can change what our future may hold, but with God's help we can refuse to focus on the negative, and instead, focus on the blessings God brings into our lives. It requires a conscious choice to do this, and it's a choice I need to make every day in order for my life to emulate hope, victory, and love.

Dear Lord, In the stillness of this time with You, help me make the choice to see myself as You do, not someone with faults, failures, or inabilities. Help me see the unique creation You have made and the purpose You have for my life in this season and place. I desire to feel Your joy and choose to live with purpose each day. Amen

Distraction of Devastation

> *So do not fear, for I am with you; do not be dismayed, for I am your God, I will strengthen you and help you; I will uphold you with my righteous right hand.*
> — Isaiah 41:10

Watching the news can be spiritually exhausting, especially when I see the tragedy of human loss at the hands of another person or the complete devastation of an area due to natural disasters like tornados, hurricanes, earthquakes, and fire. Recently a town near me was completely destroyed by flood. Both crime and weather disasters have no pattern, rhyme, or reason. The loss and damage takes years to repair and rebuild. In most situations, there is no returning to normalcy but only establishing a new normal.

Many of us may never face a large devastation such as a hurricane or a tsunami, but the losses we experience can be just as devastating and life changing. Some are mere detours keeping us off our familiar routine, and with time, our schedules and relationships recover and return to normal. Other losses devastate our world with the force of a tsunami, robbing us of possessions, identity, and intimate relationships. These are the mornings when we open our eyes and realize; normal will never be the same again.

Many times I will use the image of a smashed cup when I speak about life's hardships. I don't mean just cracked, chipped, or broken, but smashed into tiny smithereens with no possible way to re-glue or repair it to its original shape. It is these times that God reaches down to gently and lovingly pick up each piece and hold them in His hands. You see when life is broken, God doesn't just glue the pieces back together. With time, healing, love, comfort, and strength, He works in our lives to recreate new masterpieces. This process is never easy and many times we only see the brokenness. We become frustrated and cry out to God, "How much longer?" God's promises in scripture never guarantee us a time line, but assure us that we are not alone.

So do not fear, for I am with you; do not be dismayed, for I am your God, I will strengthen you and help you; I will uphold you with my righteous right hand, Isaiah 41:10.

Our Lord knows what we will encounter before we are even aware of the changes ahead. He is always there when devastation hits even if it doesn't feel like it.

In Nika Maples book, *Hunting Hope*, she describes our Lord watching over us before devastation strikes.

"The night before your world changed, you had been busy about your day with an effortless smile, laying your tired body down to rest that evening. Then the Lord knelt beside your bed, looking on with tenderness. With a gentle hand He touched your face and whispered with pain in

his eyes. Saying, Tomorrow, Tomorrow when it happens, I will be with you, I will never leave you or forsake you." Nika Maples, Hunting Hope ©2016

What are you facing today my friend? Our Lord knows your deepest hurt, your deepest loss, your deepest fears, and promises that He will never leave you or forsake you. ♥

> When life is broken, God doesn't just glue the pieces back together, He works in our lives to recreate new masterpieces. —Peg Arnold

*Dear Lord,
Sometimes the energy
to just face a new day is
overwhelming. How do I feel
Your strength? How do I find
You in the rubble of devastation,
loss, and pain that surround me?
Help me realize that when I am
on my knees tearfully picking up
the pieces of my shattered life, You are
with me, giving me strength, holding
me up and whispering "Fear not
my precious child, I am with you,
I am holding you with My
righteous right hand and
will never let you go."
Amen*

Distraction of DIY

> *They devoted themselves to the apostles' teaching and to fellowship, to the breaking of bread and to prayer.*
> — Acts 2:42

Do It Yourself (DIY) projects are everywhere! You see them in magazines, stores, on web-sites, and TV. In fact, complete networks are dedicated to DIY projects. People appear to be consumed by the vast opportunities these projects offer. Each one includes a list of explicit directions, necessary equipment, tools, and time requirements. Sometimes you will be provided a step-by-step video or photo map. If the project is remodeling or repurposing, before and after photos are often included.

I love watching the DIY shows on TV and can get lost in perusing the possibilities on the web. I marvel at the creativity of the numerous projects and the simplicity of the process. Many of the videos make the process appear foolproof and easy. Often I am inspired to attempt a project or two. However, when I attempt it, it is complicated and time consuming. Thus my basement is full of craft equipment and unfinished DIY endeavors.

I have questioned why I run into such difficulties with these projects? First of all, when I watch a video, the creator has a designated work space with all the necessary equipment collected, purchased, and organized. The filmed directions do not include searching or shopping for the items, measuring the items, etc. The 30-45 minutes demonstrated on the video takes me days, even weeks to complete. In reality, my finished project rarely resembles the beautiful picture I had the illusion of duplicating.

On the other hand, when I attempt similar projects with the support of a class, friend, or teacher to guide me through the process, my final project is much more likely to resemble the desired "after" photos. I reach a higher level of success with a little help from my friends. In other words, I am much more successful in my endeavor when I have the expertise, support, and accountability to encourage and guide me.

This made me think about my faith walk and how I approach worship, Bible study, and service. God created us to be in fellowship with others. We are responsible for our own decisions and actions, but we're not designed to function in isolation or a DIY faith. From the beginning, God did not want man to be alone and created a help-mate in Eve. The second most important commandment is relationship-oriented, and we are called to love one another as we love ourselves.

Upon reflection, I realized that my faith grows when I have the guidance, support, and encouragement of accountability partners, teachers, and leaders. Each person challenges me to look at my relationship with God and others in new ways, reveals to me the deep messages in God's word, and inspires me with their witness. Thus I grow in knowledge and faith through these relationships. Even Jesus sought the wisdom of the elders in the temple at a very young age when He knew He needed to grow.

Every one of us differs in our abilities to discipline ourselves in our faith practices, just like we differ in our creative abilities. However, God created each of us to be in relationship with one another in worship, service, and spiritual development. With my faith, I need to be discerning and endeavor to not live my faith in isolation. I am called to follow the example of the early believers who devoted themselves to the apostles' teaching, fellowship, communion, and prayer. ♥

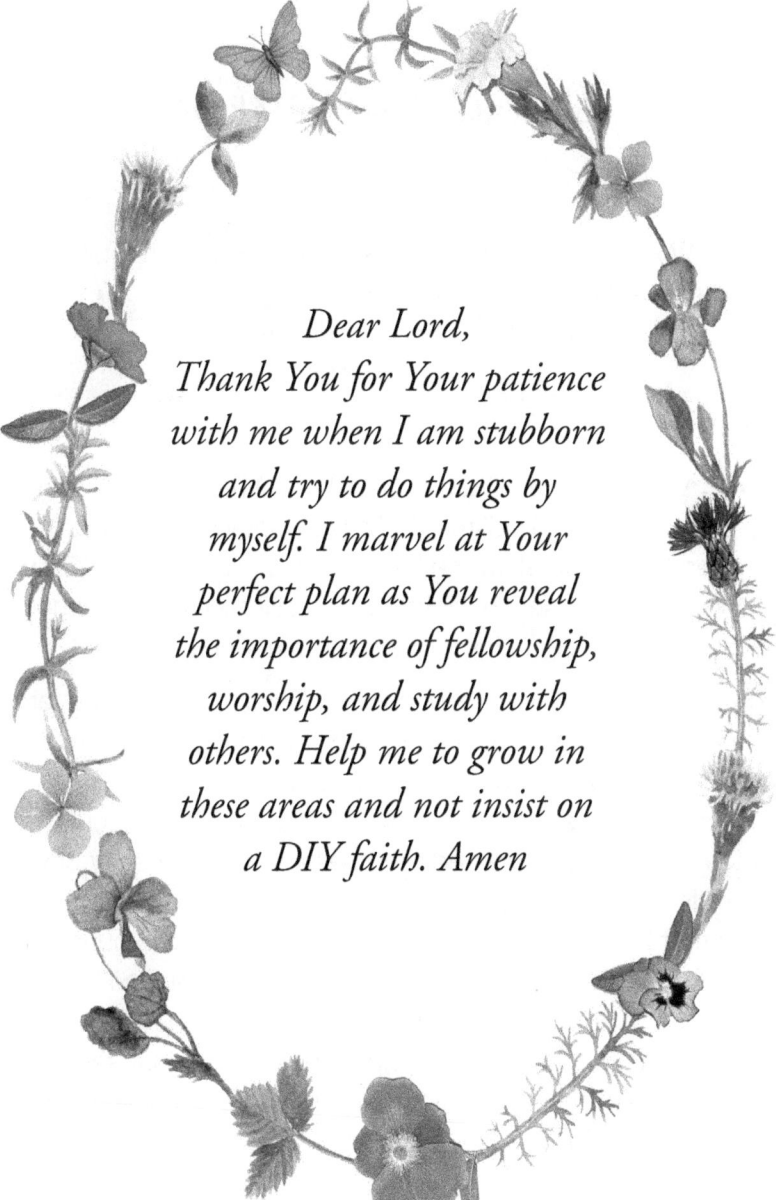

*Dear Lord,
Thank You for Your patience with me when I am stubborn and try to do things by myself. I marvel at Your perfect plan as You reveal the importance of fellowship, worship, and study with others. Help me to grow in these areas and not insist on a DIY faith. Amen*

Distraction of Darkness

> *When Jesus spoke again to the people, He said, "I am the light of the world. Whoever follows me will never walk in darkness, but will have the light of life."*
> —John 8:12

Were you ever afraid of the dark? I hated the dark as a child. At bedtime, I always wanted my door to be open enough to allow the light to shine into the room. Even though I could see the light, I would still conjure up images of monsters in the closet or alligators under the bed.

As a child, I visited Mammoth Caves in Kentucky, an intriguing maze of tunnels through the ground, some narrow and rocky, other areas large and cavernous. The stories of how they were discovered fascinated me. Throughout the tour, the guide explained the challenges of the early cave explorers including, overcoming the darkness. During this part of the tour, he turned out the light for us to experience complete darkness. Even after our eyes adjusted to the dark, it was impossible to see our own hands in front of our faces. It was an eerie experience. After what seemed like a lifetime, the guide lit a single candle, illuminating the cavernous space enough to see shadows of faces and shapes.

Distraction of Darkness

As an adult I became aware that darkness could mean more than the physical void of light. If we are not careful, spiritual darkness creeps into our lives and consumes our thoughts. Whenever Jesus references the dangers of darkness, He teaches us that, "*He is the light of the world*" and we are to carry His brightness into the world. One of my favorite childhood songs was "*This Little Light of Mine*" and I would wave my finger in the air as I sang it. This remains one of many songs encouraging us to ignite Christ's light into the lives of others. One single candle has profound power to overcome darkness.

If one small flame has the ability to light up a large cavern, how much more can Jesus illuminate the darkness in a troubled soul? Just like the candle in the cave, that single flame is a reminder of the power in Jesus' statement, *"I am the light of the world."* To access His light, how do I plug into His power? By reading scripture, Christ illuminates our mind and reveals the necessary direction in our darkness. *"Thy word is a lamp unto my feet, a light unto my path,"* Psalm 119:105. Other ways to connect to the power of Christ include prayer or seeking support of others who can shine the light into our darkness. Singing songs that remind us of God's promises or scriptures is another way to shed light upon a dark path.

Are you surrounded by darkness? Do you need to plug into the power of Christ so His light can conquer the shadows? Or are you a light bearer, able to bring Christ's light into the lives of those who need it? What is God calling

Devotions for the Distracted Heart

*Dear Lord,
Thank you for being the
Light of the World. When I
let the darkness control my
mood and overtake my spirit,
help me to seek to ignite that
small single flame of Yours
that can bring light and hope
to my soul and let it shine!
Amen*

Distraction of Discipline
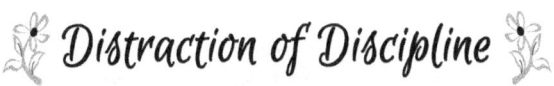

> *No act of discipline seems pleasant at the time, but painful. Later on, however, it produces a harvest of righteousness and peace for those who have been trained by it.*
> —Hebrews 12:11

When I was a young mom and heard the word "discipline" it was always associated with punishment. There were many popular parenting books with opposing beliefs about punishment and discipline. Even the mothers in my Bible study group debated this dilemma with one side citing the Bible verse, *"Whoever spares the rod hates their children, but the one who loves their children is careful to discipline them,"* Proverbs 13:24.

It was my own wise mother who expanded my definition of discipline. She worked with single mothers through the social services department, teaching them skills in the areas of cooking, cleaning, parenting, and more. She explained how these young mothers did not have healthy parenting role models. Instead, their childhoods were shaped with violence and dysfunction. The discussion of discipline came up during one session, and most of the women spoke of their abusive backgrounds. It was important for these mothers to hear that discipline was not only punishment but instruction and training. This was a new concept to them and to me.

The use of the word "discipline" is often misconstrued. True discipline is a process by which we can train ourselves and others to learn new skills and behaviors. The practice includes generating expectations and boundaries with rewards and consequences. For discipline in the home, my mom explained the importance of building a foundation of love and trust before establishing boundaries and expectations. When that foundation of love and trust is present, then the process of shaping the desired behaviors is more effective. When behaviors demonstrate respect for the boundaries and expectations, there should be a positive response. However, when the behaviors defy the boundaries or expectations, implementing a consequence that fits the disobedience is equally important.

Throughout the Bible there are verses that refer to "discipline". Each illustration implies that we grow closer in our relationship with God by adhering to His discipline. One example states, *"Blessed is the one whom God corrects; so do not despise the discipline of the Almighty,"* Job 5:17.

Discipline is a series of practices we implement in our lives on many levels, not just as parents or in our relationship with God, but in the goals we set for ourselves. Losing weight, starting new exercise routines, establishing daily devotions, or taking a class that challenges us require both discipline and commitment. I love the verse, *No act of discipline seems pleasant at the time, but painful. Later on, however, it produces a harvest of righteousness and peace for those who have been trained by it,* Hebrews 12:11. This verse explains that discipline not only has a purpose, but it requires a process. In addition, the scripture states that there is a celebrated outcome if we remain faithful and committed to its practices and expectations.

If we consider ourselves "children of God", then He is the parent who lovingly creates boundaries that will shape us into His image. We have the choice to seek His ways and grow more like Him. However, we can become distracted and easily swayed to disregard those expectations and follow the ways of the world. Which path do you desire to follow? ♥

Dear Lord, Help me to establish the habits and actions in my life that will bring me closer to walking with You and serving You each day. Rather than being fearful of Your discipline towards me, help me improve the daily disciplines that allow my heart to know Your will more deeply. Amen

Distraction of Directions

> *"For I know the plans I have for you," declares the LORD, "plans to prosper you and not to harm you, plans to give you hope and a future."*
> —Jeremiah 29:11

How do you map out a trip when you travel? I remember using the old tri-fold highway maps and running my finger over the route. Sometimes I even traced it with a pencil as we followed the directions to wherever we were going for that day. On family vacations, I loved being the "navigator" and telling the driver where to turn.

When I lived in Michigan, I became so good at mapping out trips, I could anticipate the entire route in my head. I'd picture where we would begin, the directions we would take, and the final destination! Being able to visualize where we were going gave me comfort, and if we needed a detour, I had the confidence that I could always get us back on track. When I moved to Maryland, things changed for me because I was not familiar with any of the routes. For a while I felt lost and out of control as I tried to acquaint myself with the new territory.

With all the technological advances available to us today, the use of tri-fold highway maps seems like a

Distraction of Directions

prehistoric skill. Many of us have graduated to the wonders of Mapquest, the wisdom of our GPS companions or even the whimsy of Siri. With each of these inventions, we only need to know the starting point and the address of the final destination, and our technological wizards will devise turn-by-turn directions. In some cases, we get to choose the quickest, shortest, and even the most scenic routes. Many GPS systems have a detour "app" to help design a new set of directions when traffic jams or construction have blocked the initial path.

What's the difference in using my GPS over my trusty tri-fold highway map? I find that using my technological option lures me into a blind dependence and a false sense of trust. When I had my map, I had a sense of control. I could see the roads, the terrain, the location of cities, and alternative routes. The GPS is totally different. Oh, I do have access to the complete map on a convenient 4" by 4" screen. I could take the time to acquaint myself with the entire set of directions, but do I do this?

More often, I put my faith in the satellite to find me, plug in the address of the final destination, and converse with my GPS companion, trusting her directions of "turn right in one-half mile". These directions typically work well, and I arrive at the destination without problems. But then there are the times I do not hear the directions, decide to try my own short-cut, or I take a wrong turn, and the next direction is over-ridden with the voice "recalculating". This can be very frustrating and (if riding with a companion or spouse) can be the source of stress or even conflict. Add to this the demands of a time constraint, and you have the recipe for disaster.

So how does this apply to our faith? Remember the journey of Moses: he progressed from living in the palace, to living as a nomad, and a slave. Eventually, he was raised to lead the Israelites out of Egypt. He knew that the destination was the Promised Land, and had faith that God would provide step-by-step directions. Moses did not see the overall map, but he completely trusted God to go before him leading the way..

Noah also depended upon God's directions without question. In spite of constant ridicule, he followed God's explicit instructions to build an ark. He had faith that it would be needed for the flood promised by God. There are many other Biblical examples of faithful men and women who were called by God and given a mission or a direction. All of them gave witness to God's glory when they were faithful to those directions. There are also examples of devastations encountered when God's directions were not followed. Remember the story of Jonah and the whale? In his disobedience, Jonah heard the voice of God saying "recalculating" as he tried to avoid Nineveh and instead became lunch for Moby Dick!

Were any of these saints given a complete, detailed route that revealed all of the pitfalls, storms, road blocks, or difficulties? No! God holds the tri-fold highway map and navigates for us if we take the time to listen. God Provides Step-by-step (GPS) directions to all who take time to read His word, spend time in prayer, and seek to follow His voice.

Sometimes it may seem that the Biblical characters could hear God's voice better than we can today. Don't you believe it! His voice is just as clear today as it was many

Distraction of Directions

years ago and His promises are true for us as believers. He has dreams and goals that He wants each of us to achieve. Perhaps we have more distractions that drown out His clear guidance, and if we listen to the wrong voice, we will hear God sigh and say....recalculating! Can you hear God's voice in your life? ♥

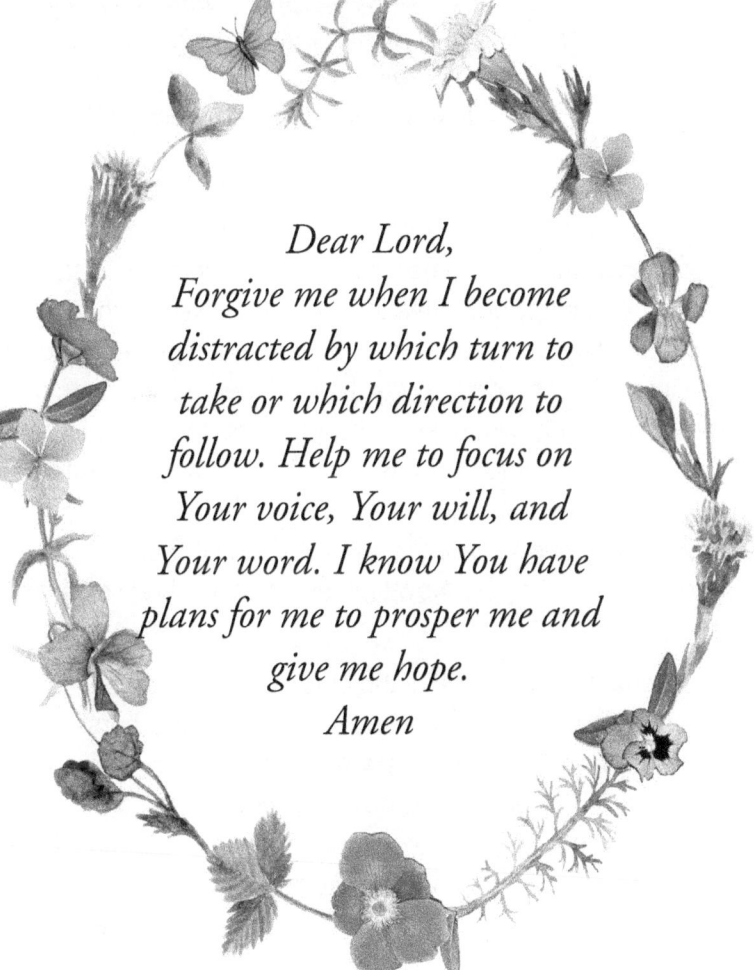

Dear Lord,
Forgive me when I become distracted by which turn to take or which direction to follow. Help me to focus on Your voice, Your will, and Your word. I know You have plans for me to prosper me and give me hope.
Amen

Distraction of Dementia

> *The Lord is good to those whose hope is in him, to the one who seeks him; it is good to wait quietly for the salvation of the Lord.*
>
> —Lamentations 3:25–26

As I sat there feeding lunch to my mother, I was savoring our moments together. Living out of state, I had very few opportunities to visit and serve her in such a poignant way. The one-sided conversation was responded to with smiles and a few nods. I reminisced about the things we used to do when she visited us in the Washington, D.C. area. Her eyes lit up as I described cherry blossoms, touring the monuments, and other special activities. My mother was once a vibrant, wise woman who cared for me and gave me support. Now time and disease have reversed those roles.

During this meal, one of the nurses came over to give my mother her medications. As she sat down, the nurse said, "Well, it looks like you have a guest here. Who is this nice young lady?" It was at that point my mother raised her eyes to look at me and gave me a haunting, hollow stare as if she could not place me anywhere in her memory banks. This was the first time my mother did not know who I was and

Distraction of Dementia

could not recall my name. I knew this day would come, but I then realized, one is never prepared for the day your own mother does not remember you.

I was determined to have my mother recognize me that day since I only had a few hours before catching a plane home. I took her back to her room and was certain that pictures would jar her memory. I took the family photo off the wall and pointed to my siblings as she named each one. When I pointed to my own image, she looked at me saying, "I don't know," confirming the excruciating fact that she truly did not recognize me.

My heart sank. Holding back the tears, I replied, "Mom, that's me. I'm your daughter, your third daughter."

She shook her head and questioned, "Why don't I remember?" I responded with a kiss and assured her that she would remember someday, as I knew this was beyond her control. Then I changed the subject and continued to reminisce about activities we did together and sing some familiar songs. This always brought a smile to her face and eventually she fell asleep.

The journey you travel when a loved one has dementia is filled with many goodbyes because you lose your loved one in pieces. Sometimes the moment slips away silently, and it is only in retrospect you realize you no longer have that connection. For instance, I can't remember the last time I spoke to my mom on the phone. I knew our conversations were becoming disjointed and difficult, but soon the moment was lost and only remains a memory. Sometimes the good-bye rips at your heart as the loss is one more reminder that there is no turning back from this deteriorating disease.

    My mother went to be with the Lord in 2012, yet I'm still distracted and grieved by these memories. My prayers go out to anyone who may have traveled or is traveling this same journey. I find comfort in the words from Lamentations 3. For no matter how difficult things are, the author of this scripture reminds me to put my hope in the Lord. *My soul is downcast within me. Yet this I call to mind and therefore I have hope,* Lamentations 3:20–21. It is this foundation of faith and hope that supported and comforted both of my parents through the challenging years of dementia and aging losses. It is this same hope that comforts me. *The Lord is good to those whose hope is in him, to the one who seeks him; it is good to wait quietly for the salvation of the Lord,* Lamentations 3:25–26.

    As I remember my mom, I will not let the challenges of dementia distract me from the loving memories of her final years. Instead I will celebrate her vitality, gifts, love, and legacy of faith, for throughout her life she put her hope in the Lord. ♥

Distraction of Dementia

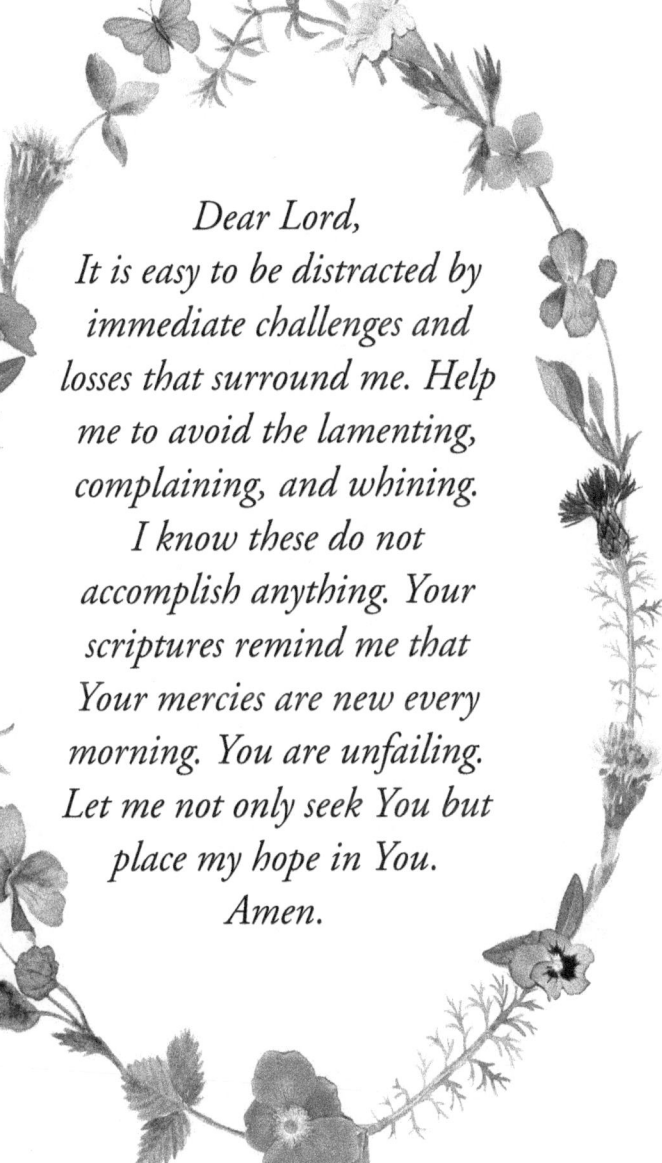

Dear Lord,
It is easy to be distracted by immediate challenges and losses that surround me. Help me to avoid the lamenting, complaining, and whining.
I know these do not accomplish anything. Your scriptures remind me that Your mercies are new every morning. You are unfailing. Let me not only seek You but place my hope in You.
Amen.

Distraction of Dialogue

> *Let your conversation always be seasoned with grace,
> so you may know how to answer everyone.*
> —Colossians 4:6

Dialogue is defined as a conversation between two people. The dialogue can be a sharing of ideas, plans, hopes, dreams, memories, and more. But as the definition states, this communication occurs between two parties; a sender and a receiver. Dialogue refers to the actual verbal words that are shared in a conversation.

If you have read any articles about communication, you know that the non-verbal cues impact the exchange of information far more significantly than the spoken word. Albert Mehrabian is one of the first researchers who divided communication channels into three areas; body language, tone of voice and actual dialogue. In his research (Mehrabian, A., Communication model, 1972) he discovered that the majority of communication is expressed through the non-verbal modalities of body language (55%) and tone of voice (38%), leaving 7% for the actual dialogue. If this is true, then by increasing awareness of our mood, tone, and gestures, we can increase the ability to

Distraction of Dialogue

communicate more effectively. The actual dialogue is only a portion of the message.

How does this relate to our dialogues with God? If we are the sender, we communicate with our words, songs, actions, thoughts, intentions, and more. He doesn't need the body language or the tone of voice because He sees beyond our words to the true heart of our message. He knows if we are being shallow, fleeting, sincere, or hurting. Proverbs 21:2 from the Message says, *"We justify our actions by appearances, God examines our motives."* Have you thought about your personal dialogues with your Savior? How often do you talk with Him? What are your motives? Do you share expressions of adoration, gratitude, and confession, or are most of your prayers filled with requests for your needs and the needs of others?

More importantly, how does God communicate back to us? Remember communication involves both sending and receiving the message. How does God speak to you? I marvel at the experiences of people who actually hear the voice of God. Moses and many other characters in the Bible heard the voice of God. My own mother shared a very moving story of hearing the audible voice of God. But I don't think God frequently uses this mode of communication. Since we communicate with dialogue, I believe God speaks to us through our senses. He may use other believers to be His messengers for us. Many times people are not even aware they are carriers of the divine message, but when the receiver hears the words, it is clear that it's the voice of God.

There are various other channels of communication our loving Lord uses to speak to us. I hear God's voice in nature: the beauty of a sunrise, the visit of a hummingbird, the fragrance of a spring day, or the majesty of a landscape. I hear God speaking to me through scripture. The same scripture read at a different time, can communicate a different message, depending on my own circumstances. I hear the voice of God through music. Whether it has words or not the spirit can transport my emotions to deep places of conviction. I hear God in times of weakness as He woos me to depend on Him. Finally, I hear the voice of God through quiet meditation. It's difficult to do this in our world filled with many distractions. By intentionally seeking the Spirit in the still moments, I sense connection and receive peace, communicated without words.

So the next time you are in a prayer dialogue with God, remember, communication is a two way street. He is speaking to you from a myriad of modalities; just take the time to listen. Remember as you pray, He does not require you to fill the space with dialogue. He does not want you worrying about tone of voice or body language. He will hear your heart. If you listen purposely, He has a message of unending love, comfort, strength, and peace. ♥

Distraction of Dialogue

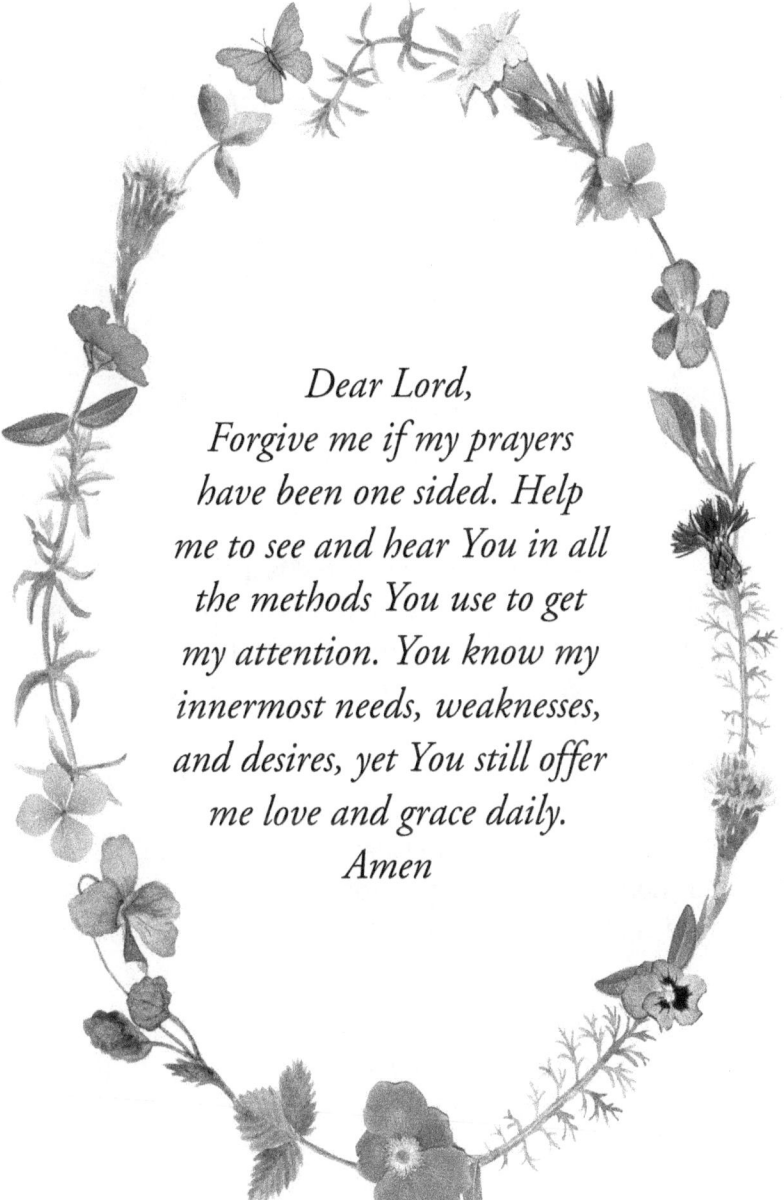

Dear Lord,
Forgive me if my prayers have been one sided. Help me to see and hear You in all the methods You use to get my attention. You know my innermost needs, weaknesses, and desires, yet You still offer me love and grace daily.
Amen

Distraction of Discontent

> *I know what it is to be in need, and I know what it is to have plenty. I have learned the secret of being content in any and every situation, whether well fed or hungry, whether living in plenty or in want. I can do all this through Him who gives me strength.*
> —Philippians 4:12–13

I will be happy when, complete this statement. When I have my debts paid? When I lose 15 pounds? When I have a new job? When I move? When I am in a new relationship? When? Contentment defined in Webster's dictionary is *"a feeling experienced when one's wishes are met."* Bing defines it as *"a feeling of calm satisfaction"*. Many times we associate contentment or satisfaction with our level of happiness. So what makes you happy? What brings contentment? Is it ever possible to reach the defined state of contentment without having all your wishes fulfilled?

When my husband lost his job the first time, I was working part time, and we had a child heading off to college. Could I ever find contentment in these circumstances? No matter where we are in life there will always be challenges to overcome. These can come in the form of day-to-day stresses, financial demands, work problems, and relationship issues, not to mention illnesses, losses and the unexpected events that consume our energies and challenge our emotions. Add to this, media messages that upset us with world tragedies or product messages designed to lure us into a state of discontent.

So is Webster right? Is true contentment only reached when all our desires have been met? I sure hope not. Compare the Webster's dictionary definition to Paul's insights on contentment. He writes in Philippians 4:12, *"I know what it is to be in need, and I know what it is to have plenty. I have learned the secret of being content in any and every situation, whether well fed or hungry, whether living in plenty or in want."* Paul's level of contentment or satisfaction exists in spite of his circumstances. This is in deep contrast to the worldly definition of contentment which depends upon the fulfillment of our needs and desires.

There are many modern authors and personalities who support the idea that contentment is based on an inner state of mind (positive mindset) rather than an external state of circumstances. Paul's deep faith in the sovereignty, compassion, and omniscience of our Lord Jesus Christ is far more significant than just a positive mindset. In the very next verse, Philippians 4:13, Paul writes, *"I can do all things through Christ who strengthens me."* Paul has no doubt Who defines him, in Whom he finds his identity, and Who lifts him up beyond his circumstances. This is the true secret to contentment; identity in Christ who gives us peace in spite of our circumstances.

During my husband's unemployment, we received blessings beyond our expectation. It was a time filled with struggles, but not a time of discontent. Sometimes we can fall into the trap of measuring the contentment of our souls by our achievements, possessions, or positive relationships. Many of these things can bring joy and celebration to our lives. But true contentment does not come from the day to day successes or even challenges. Each of us is a valued God-gifted creation, with insights and abilities to be used for His purposes. Our relationship with Him, and learning to love ourselves and others as He loves us, is the secret to true peace, internal joy, and contentment. ♥

*Dear Lord,
Help me to find true peace and contentment in my relationship with You. Like Paul, I want to be content in all circumstances. No matter the challenges that may face me, You my Lord are the one who defines me and the only one who satisfies my soul.
Amen*

Distraction of Dependence

> *In the same way, the Spirit helps us in our weakness. We do not know what we ought to pray for, but the Spirit himself intercedes for us through wordless groans. And he who searches our hearts knows the mind of the Spirit, because the Spirit intercedes for God's people in accordance with the will of God.*
> —Romans 8:26–27

With my mother's Parkinson's and dementia came limitations that made her dependent on external help for everything. I marveled at how my dad sacrificially cared for her, feeding her meals, going to events, and even ordering an accessible van for a special birthday meal with the family. I knew these days were difficult, yet he often spoke of the privilege of being able to serve and care for her. I truly felt his example embodied how Christ cares for us.

Fast forward several years and I find myself having to ask others for help with simple personal tasks following an injury requiring surgery. My situation is temporary, but I often think of Mom and other friends whose confinement and limitations were permanent. For me, this has been a humbling experience. Simple tasks I had taken for granted

Distraction of Dependence

cannot be done without a request, inconveniencing someone else. It was one thing to disrupt the routines of my family, but when in public, I found myself relying on the kindness of strangers for things like opening a door or picking up something I dropped.

This experience has made me truly appreciate having a healthy body. It has also given me time to reflect on my dependency on God. In this state of physical brokenness, I am fully dependent on the support of others to get through each day. When I am not injured, I am an independent person and able to reach out to help others. What does this reveal about my relationship and trust in God?

I realized the idea of being dependent on God is easy to say, but much harder to put into practice. I remember times when we experienced unemployment causing us to truly depend on God for our basic needs. During those struggles, we spent time in His word and sought Him daily. However, once work was secured with a regular paycheck, our schedules became busy again. Unfortunately, this resulted in losing some of the intimacy we had been sharing with the Lord during our time of need.

I recognized I had to depend on others when I was physically broken. It made me question if I was depending on God only when spiritually broken? The scripture in Romans 8 tells me that God is there to help me in those times of weakness and brokenness, interceding for me when I don't know how to pray.

In the same way, the Spirit helps us in our weakness. We do not know what we ought to pray for, but the Spirit himself

Devotions for the Distracted Heart

intercedes for us through wordless groans. And he who searches our hearts knows the mind of the Spirit, because the Spirit intercedes for God's people in accordance with the will of God, Romans 8:26–27.

As I gain more independence in the healing process, I do not want my awareness of this dependency on God to fade. My desire is to be intentional with my daily devotions and seek His will for strength and guidance. It is my prayer that I will be mindful of others at home and in public. People have reached out to support me during my time of need, so I want to return that same spirit of giving. What about you? Do you live your life independently, or are you truly dependent on God, whether you're in times of brokenness or abundance? ♥

Distraction of Dependence

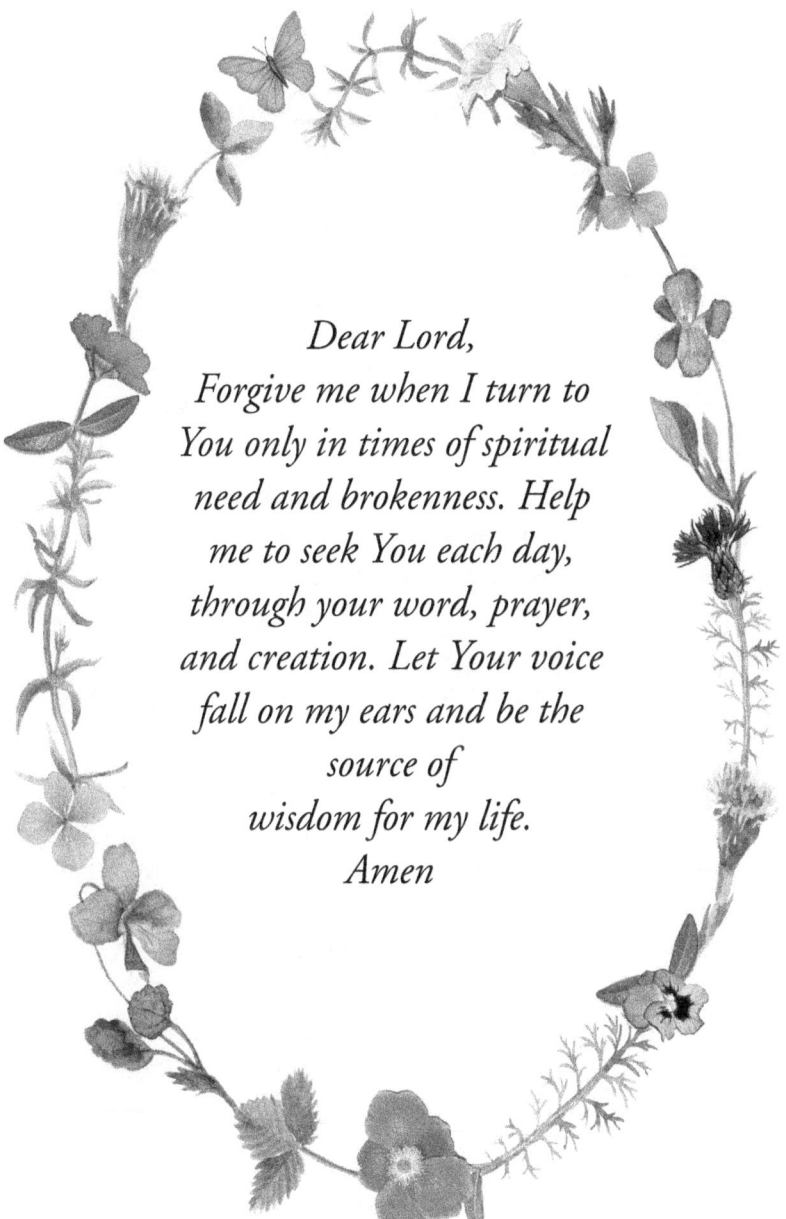

*Dear Lord,
Forgive me when I turn to
You only in times of spiritual
need and brokenness. Help
me to seek You each day,
through your word, prayer,
and creation. Let Your voice
fall on my ears and be the
source of
wisdom for my life.
Amen*

Distraction of Denali

> *Though you have not seen him, you love him; and even though you do not see him now, you believe in him and are filled with an inexpressible and glorious joy.*
> —1 Peter 1:8

A few years ago I had the incredible opportunity to go to Alaska. I was with my husband, my siblings and their spouses. Each day surrounded us with new sights and breath-taking scenes of God's creation. We were blessed with mountain vistas, expansive glaciers, fascinating wild life, including a trip to the Arctic Circle. What a fabulous experience!

If you have ever traveled this route, you know that stopping at Denali National Park is one of the highlights. Our itinerary included a stop-over in a quaint little town called Talkeetna. Our hotel boasted that, on a clear day, you could see the highest peak in North America, Mt McKinley, otherwise known as, Denali. The key phrase is "on a clear day". We were at this hotel for three days and two nights. We had hoped that we might see the mountain even though it was only visible 30% of the time.

As we entered the hotel, we were surrounded with pictures, murals, and even relief models of the grand mountain. We walked out to the observation deck which was lined with chairs facing the north, yet we saw nothing. Throughout the hotel there was no shortage of books and stories about Mt McKinley, and yet each morning we would rise and look to the north, still no mountain in sight, not even foothills.

Our final day in Talkeetna, the sun came out and the clouds began to clear. The excitement was infectious as people flocked to the observation deck and cameras clicked. The sight was beautiful with the snow-capped mountains in the distance. But the enthusiasm died down when a hotel staff informed the crowd that the landscape being photographed was only the foothills and the "High One" was not visible. We felt cheated and began doubting if we would ever experience the sight of this magnificent peak, but we did not give up. We continued to search the horizon for the treasured view of Denali.

Do you ever feel that way about God? You know He exists, you hear of His faithfulness and mighty works from others. You read stories about Him, but in your life it seems as though He is not there. Whether you feel God's presence or not you can be sure He is always present, and He loves and cares for you.

1 Peter talks about the reward that we receive when we continue to be faithful to God. *Though you have not seen him, you love him; and even though you do not see him now, you believe in him and are filled with an inexpressible and glorious joy.* Not only will we encounter an inexpressible joy, but we will receive salvation for our souls in exchange for our unfailing belief.

Did we ever get a glimpse of this incredible mountain? Yes, but only for a brief moment. We were touring the National park when the clouds finally cleared and exposed the Denali peak in all its magnificent glory. Isn't that like our Lord? When the clouds of challenges clear, we finally see the amazing way that God has always been in our midst caring and protecting us all along the way.

*Dear Lord,
Even though I don't see You some days or feel Your presence, help me to believe without doubt to receive Your inexpressible joy and the gift of salvation. These are gifts that only come from You because Your presence abides and remains within me.
Amen.*

Distraction of Despair

> *From the depths of despair,*
> *O Lord, I call for your help.*
> —Psalm 130:1

My heart is heavy each time I hear about another famous person taking his life. It's a reminder that true peace and identity are not found in money, fame, or success. There is something more powerful and dangerous that haunts a human soul and shrouds it from true contentment. For some it is shame, despair, or loneliness, yet each of these can lead to a dark hole where there is no hope. Some of you may have experienced this in your own lives going through the shock and horror of a loss in your family or circle of friends. Suicide is now the second highest cause of death for several age groups. So I am asking, how do we make a difference and stop this senseless loss?

First, we each need to be courageous enough to break through the 'Fine' facade. You know the one I am referring to. 'How are you?' 'Fine.' Many people work diligently creating a "put-together" appearance while fighting to hide their vulnerabilities from the world. Is it possible to take the time to peer into their eyes, and be that shoulder to cry on?

To be like Jesus and love with His agape love, letting them know there is someone who cares?

I know this is not the answer for every circumstance. Some require professional help, but sometimes I think we use this as an excuse. Each of us has the ability to be a vessel of hope for the hopeless. In the first and greatest commandment God calls us to *"love the Lord your God with all your heart, all your soul, and all your mind.'* A second commandment is equally important; *'Love your neighbor as yourself.'* Matthew 22:37-39. This means that establishing authentic relationships that reach beyond the façade of "fine" must be a priority for us as Christians.

So how do we become vessels of HOPE?

Hear, by taking the time to really listen. When you ask that question, "How are you?" hear the answer with your heart. They may need your listening ear.

Open your arms – Touching has the power to remove that sense of isolation. But physical contact without expectations may be a foreign concept to some people. Thus before I hold a hand, give a hug, or even touch a shoulder, I ask for permission.

Pray for guidance and wisdom as you respond. God will give you the words to pray appropriately for the situation.

Encourage with words – There is no formula for this conversation. It is important to listen and accept them right where they are, providing hope for their situation. If necessary, connect them with a pastor or other for professional support.

Remember, God created us to be in relationship with Him and each other. Everyone can be a beacon of hope for someone in despair if we listen with our hearts and reach beyond the 'façade of fine.' ♥

Dear Lord,
Use me as a vessel of
HOPE in the lives of those in
need. You have given me gifts to
relate to different people. Help me
to Hear, Open, Pray, and
Encourage. Some reading this right
now may be suffering and need Your
arms around them. I am calling
out to You to send help, guidance,
strength, and answers. I lift
this to You, our loving God.
Amen.

Distraction of Diets

> *But the Lord said to Samuel, Look not on his appearance or at the height of his stature, for I have rejected him. For the Lord sees not as man sees; for man looks on the outward appearance, but the Lord looks on the heart.*
> —1 Samuel 16:7

Fat free, gluten free, carb free, lactose free, nut free, sugar free, whether you are trying to lose weight, eat healthier, control allergies, or gain weight, there is a diet for everyone. You cannot go through the aisle of any grocery store without seeing claims of wonder foods that reduce the signs of aging, improve your mood, give you more energy, or help you lose weight. The enticements are everywhere. Some of them are outlandish promises, and yet there are many programs that teach healthy habits, nutrition, and meal planning which can lead to an improved you!

I have to admit that I have been on more diets than I can count. I have lost the same pounds over and over, only to gain them back. The older I get, the more difficult this fight becomes. I once heard a speaker sum up the difficulty of losing weight as we grow older. She said something like, "I used to lose a couple pounds just by skipping lunch, now I have to skip January!"

Distraction of Diets

Why do some of us become so consumed with the number on the scale, our image in the mirror, or the size of our clothing? If it is not weight or age we are distracted by, it might be another physical feature with which we struggle. One of the main reasons for this obsession is that we live in a visually oriented society. Our world tends to measure everything by appearances, and we fall victim to that same trap.

As I searched the scriptures for answers, I never found any spiritual reference about going on a diet to lose weight. There were examples and laws about fasting: what, how, and even when to eat, but, no reference to losing weight. In fact, the purpose was for repentance, sacrifice, or growing closer in one's relationship with God. There were no examples of God's rejection for a person's weight or appearance. In fact I found the opposite.

Remember the story about Samuel going to the house of Jesse to look for a replacement for King Saul? Jesse had many sons, and he brought each one of them to Samuel. One by one, whether tall, strong, or capable, to Jesse's dismay, each one was rejected. 1st Samuel 16:7 says *"But the Lord said to Samuel, Look not on his appearance or at the height of his stature, for I have rejected him. For the Lord sees not as man sees; for man looks on the outward appearance, but the Lord looks on the heart.* David was the last son brought forth. Because he was Jesse's youngest, smallest, and weakest son, he did not consider him a candidate, but David was the Lord's anointed one.

Man looks on the outward appearance, but God looks at the heart. Do you get distracted by measuring yourself

Devotions for the Distracted Heart

with the number on the scales or expectations of the world? This scripture tells you that you are created special in His eyes, no matter if you are weak, strong, old, young, heavy, thin, rich, or poor. God sees your heart and anoints you as worthy.

So close your eyes to those messages that tell you what you need to look like, weigh, eat, act, or wear. You are loved by our Creator and are special in His eyes.

Dear Lord, Thank you for this reminder that You see my heart, personal desires, and You love me unconditionally. Help me to focus more on my inward strengths and abilities than be distracted by my outward appearance. Amen.

Distraction of Deterioration

> *You are like whitewashed tombs, which look beautiful on the outside but on the inside are full of the bones of the dead and everything unclean.*
> —Matthew 23:27

Have you ever watched the shows on HGTV where a home is redesigned and remodeled in the course of one hour? Typically a list of improvements is agreed upon and a budget is set. When the demolition begins, there is always an unexpected, potentially dangerous complication revealed behind the original walls. I always thought this was part of the "scripted reality", until we encountered a similar challenge.

We originally thought we were going to be replacing our windows. Then the project morphed into much more when we discovered the years of deteriorating wood due to water leakage. We thought we were only going to be upgrading our insulation until we discovered years of damage from the inhabitance of snakes, mice, and bees in our walls. Unlike the one hour television show, we lived in our construction changes for about nine months. Instead of being treated to an alternative living space, we suffered through the challenges of dry wall dust and remodeling confusion.

During this process, I was amazed at the number of hidden issues we found buried behind our intact painted and decorated walls. It reminded me of the scripture from the gospels where Christ is accusing the Pharisees of hypocritical attitudes. *You are like whitewashed tombs, which look beautiful on the outside but on the inside are full of the bones of the dead and everything unclean,* Matthew 23:27. Then I began to wonder, "Can I fall into this same trap as well? I surely don't want to be seen as a hypocrite, but are there times that I worry more about the outer physical appearance than the inward spiritual condition?"

Do we work to keep up our outer appearance as a barrier protecting the secrets of our inner spirit? As believers we are encouraged to reflect and remove any walls we may be building. It is important to identify the areas of spiritual deterioration, begin the process of cleaning out, and seek healing for the damage where needed. These can be areas of insecurity, jealousy, guilt, pride, unforgiveness, and anything else that we hold onto tightly. Left alone, these scars and hurts have the potential to weaken our spirit and deteriorate our relationships. Christ loves us and offers to help us clean out anything that may be lurking in our spirit, we only need to ask. ♥

Distraction of Deterioration

*Dear Lord,
Create in me a clean heart
and renew a steadfast spirit
within me. Cast me not
away from Your presence
Lord and take not Your
spirit from me. Restore unto
me, the joy of thy salvation,
and renew a right spirit
within me.
Amen.
(Prayer from
Psalm 51:10–12)*

Distraction of Death

> *There is a time for everything and a season for every activity under the heavens: a time to be born and a time to die, a time to weep and a time to laugh, a time to mourn and a time to dance,*
> —Ecclesiastes 3:1–2, 4

Losing someone we love can be devastating. Each death we experience puts us on our own path of grief and looks different with each loss. Occasionally, there are untimely deaths that don't just detour us but completely destroy the road we are on, changing "normal" forever. I pray the following reflection will offer comfort to those who are in different stages of loss, grief and rebuilding their lives. The Lord gave me this refection after I lost my Mom.

"He has sent me (Isaiah) to bind up the brokenhearted, to comfort all who mourn," Isaiah 61:1b–2 .

The Garments of Grief – by Peg Arnold 2012

Death is the ruthless thief that rips away a vibrant spirit at the most unexpected time.

Death is the uninvited visitor that lurks in the corners and leaves with a precious soul in spite of the prayers for healing.

The Distraction of Death

Death is the expected and sometimes welcome guest that escorts a loved one up the golden stairway to their heavenly Savior.

Whether you experience death as the thief, the uninvited visitor, or the guest, Death leaves a wardrobe of grief garments, for those who remain behind.

The quilt of memories offers a refuge in the lonely times and sometimes lulls you back to sleep on those mornings it is hard to move.

The scratchy undergarment of despair makes every task difficult, yet there is no easy way to remove it in exchange for another garment.

The hooded sweatshirt of avoidance, covers your head and allows you to escape from connecting with others and continue on as if nothing has happened.

The shoes of shock provide a deceitful opportunity to run away from the truth of death.

The black shawl of sorrow exposes your grief and loss to everyone you know.

The heavy coat appears normal, but everywhere you go, you carry the invisible, weighted burden of loss.

The healing robe is like a hug and provides security at the end of an exhausting day.

The wristwatch of time marks celebrations and memories as a constant reminder of the permanency of the loss of your loved one.

The mask of cheer conceals your anger, loneliness and tears from the world, letting you pretend that everything is okay.

The suit of acceptance, hides in the back corner. You look at it now and then, but each time you try it on, it doesn't fit quite right, yet.

Each garment is neatly stored in the wardrobe that Death leaves, and it's normal for us to wear any one of these garments throughout our grief process.

Some garments we choose to wear, other times the garment chooses us.

Some garments lose their usefulness early, but others linger in the corners, and we are caught by surprise when they appear.

The one garment that Jesus offers to us every morning is the garment of praise instead of a spirit of despair. It is a promise of heaven's gift of reunion for all those who believe in Jesus Christ.

Isaiah the prophet reassures us that the Lord, *"provides for those who grieve in Zion, to bestow on them a crown of beauty instead of ashes, the oil of joy instead of mourning, and a garment of praise instead of a spirit of despair,"* Isaiah 61:3.

Dear Lord,
As I rise each morning and go to bed each night, help me to seek Your strength, comfort, and wisdom in this season of grief. I thank You for my loved one's life, his/her gifts, faith, and legacy. I pray for those I know who are also walking this difficult path of grief. Surround them with comfort and strength to face each day.
Amen

Distraction of Ducks

> *My dear brothers and sisters, take note of this: Everyone should be quick to listen, slow to speak and slow to become angry.*
> —James 1:19

As the car cruised through the tree-canopied country road, my husband and I were savoring the unusual warmth of the early spring day. Mini rivers of melting snow were running down the hillsides, pooling in the troughs on either side of the road. We were enjoying this stolen moment at the end of a busy work day, each lost in our own thoughts until we passed an old farmhouse.

"Did you see those ducks?" my husband asked.

"Ducks? They were chickens!" I replied.

"No honey, I am talking about the mama duck with the three ducklings!'

"You mean the mama hen and the three chicks!"

"Honey, they were waddling with orange beaks!"

"Oh come on," I said. "They had yellow beaks with red crests and were pecking like this," while I moved my head up and down.

Distraction of Ducks

Believe it or not, this conversation continued for the next three miles and deteriorated to the point that I shouted, " I am not a stupid woman! I know the difference between a duck and a chicken!"

"Then I am turning this car around because I can't believe you think you saw chickens!"

"Good!" I answered. "Because I CAN'T believe you think they were ducks."

As we crested the hill, the farmhouse came into view, and I pointed up the hill to the yard in front of the porch. "SEE, those ARE chickens!" At the same time, my husband was pointing to the roadside gully saying "SEE, those ARE ducks!" Indeed, in the same yard, a mama duck with three ducklings played in the water by the side of the road and up near the farmhouse, a mama hen pecked the ground with her three baby chicks following suit. We immediately broke into uncontrollable laughter and pulled to the side of the road to gain our composure. We had been bickering for ten minutes over something on which we were both correct!

Understandably, my husband's perspective had been restricted to the road ahead while driving. My own perspective had broadened beyond the sides of the road and stretched to the horizon.

How many times do disagreements occur because of different perspectives? Both parties are correct, but fail or even refuse to see the situation through the eyes of the other one.

James reminds us in his letter to be *"quick to listen, slow to speak, and slow to get angry,"* James 1:19.

My husband and I could have chosen to continue to argue and accuse each other of being quite mistaken in what we each observed. Instead, we decided to take the time to turn around and retrace where we had been in order to increase our understanding of the situation.

I think this is what James is advising us to do when we disagree. Be slow to anger. It's easy to get mad when things do not meet our expectations or when someone disagrees with us. If we follow James' advice, be quick to listen, then we will take time to understand what the other person is saying, what their perspective is, and the past experiences that may be influencing their viewpoint. *Slow to speak* reminds us to think about what we have heard before we say something. It takes time for our brains to process different viewpoints, and many times we do not allow enough time to do this. When we are angry, we tend to react with a *fight or flight* response. Being slow to speak enables us to take a deep breath and pause before we react. It gives our brains time to shift gears from reactionary to reasoning mode.

Not every disagreement is as easy to solve as our ducks and chickens experience. But to this day, my husband and I end many conflicts by agreeing to disagree. I'll say, "It's a chicken," to which he will reply, "It's a duck". Each of us is willing to compromise as we consider the different perspectives of the other and realize that both of us CAN be right. This has taught us in a very real way that not every disagreement has a single solution. God calls us to work out our conflicts with wisdom and love. Do you have any disagreements distracting you? ♥

*Dear Lord,
In James' letter, You
remind us to be slow to anger.
Help me to remember this
when faced with a disagreement.
Help me to take the time to listen
- really listen without judging,
planning my debated answer, or
focusing on my expectations. Then
give me the wisdom and strength
to be slow to speak after I have
listened. Gently remind me that
I do not always have to have the
last word, and that some
conflicts must end
in a compromise.
Amen.*

Distraction of Displacement

So, friends, take a firm stand, feet on the ground and head high. Keep a tight grip on what you were taught. May Jesus himself and God our Father, who reached out in love and surprised you with gifts of unending help and confidence, put a fresh heart in you, invigorate your work, enliven your speech. —2 Thessalonians 2:15–17 MSG

When I was a little girl learning how to cook, my mother taught me to measure hard shortening by using the method of displacement. We filled a 4 cup measure with 3 cups water and submerged the shortening in the water until it hit the 4 cup measure line. You may remember using this method in science class when you measured the mass of an object. As a young baker, many times this process created a mess. Sometimes the shortening stuck to the sides of the measuring glass. Sometimes the water overflowed because of having too much of the greasy, white stuff on the spoon. No matter what happened, eventually I was able to measure out the exact amount of shortening, combine the other ingredients, and put my creation in the oven to bake. The process of going from a single ingredient to a mouthwatering morsel did not occur without work, but the results were typically wonderful.

Displacement occurs in each of our lives in different ways. Sometimes we are displaced geographically, having to move for a variety of reasons. Sometimes displacement is not a physical move, but a change in our status, creating a sense of wandering in our souls. This can be caused by major life events such as divorce, death, unemployment, illness, or another life event. These types of losses challenge our core identity and displace us from the realm of comfort and familiarity into a place of grief and pain.

Just like the recipe, there are numerous factors that influence our sense of displacement. If it is an anticipated move, it can be exciting as we prepare, plan, and pack to provide a smooth transition to our new surroundings. These displacements are like that perfect delectable dessert that goes together beautifully and turns out like the picture in the cookbook. On the contrary, if we are unexpectedly thrown into the situation that displaces us out of our comfort zone, we may find ourselves wandering without a familiar place in sight.

There are many Biblical examples of displacement assuring us of God's constant love, care, and protection. There was Joseph who was forced out of his family by his brothers. They did not care whether good or harm came to him, but Joseph told them *You intended to harm me, but God intended it for good,* Genesis 50:20a. Remember Shadrach, Meshach, and Abednego? King Nebuchadnezzar displaced them by throwing them into the fiery furnace because they refused to worship his golden idols. Yet, in the heat of the oven, while they sang hymns, God revealed Himself and protected

Devotions for the Distracted Heart

them. Even the disciples, when Christ was crucified, felt extremely lost and displaced.

The shortening I measured by the water displacement method was messy and difficult. But eventually the shortening experienced a process of beating and heat that created a delectable treat. In the displacements that we experience, we may feel like we are beaten or sent through fire. We may even feel like we have lost our identities, but we are never alone. God is with us protecting and holding us through the difficult transition with a promise to give us everything we will need. Paul, in all his displacements, is the one who reminds us, *"Friends, take a firm stand, feet on the ground and head high. Keep a tight grip on what you were taught. May Jesus himself and God our Father, who reached out in love and surprised you with gifts of unending help and confidence, put a fresh heart in you, invigorate your work, enliven your speech." 2 Thessalonians 2:15–17 MSG* ♥

*Dear Lord,
Sometimes I feel displaced.
It's not anything that anyone
else would recognize, but
you see the wandering in my
soul. I pray for a fresh heart
that allows me to see the
ways You protect me. I pray
for the confidence to follow
Your guidance as You lead
me to a place of joy
and peace.
Amen*

Distraction of Detox

> *If we confess our sins, he is faithful and just and will forgive us our sins and purify us from all unrighteousness.*
> —1 John 1:9

Have you ever gotten caught up in the health trend of detoxes and cleanses? These programs are available in all forms - from fruit smoothies to vegetable soup. Typically it requires a 3-7 day commitment to the special diet designed to cleanse your body of toxins. Why try it? The experts claim that the presence of toxins in the body can cause exhaustion, illness, weight gain, and other adverse effects. Clearing these toxins increases the protection from disease giving you a sense of renewal and more energy. But implementing a detox program involves time to shop and plan. In addition it requires commitment and willpower to change your diet, depriving yourself of the foods on which you typically feast and substituting healthier options.

The Old Testament is full of cleansing rituals. Both the modern and Biblical routines have several steps requiring time to plan and execute. The modern detox cleanses your internal, physical body. Through Biblical practices, the body and mind are prepared for a deeper, spiritual encounter.

Distraction of Detox

This started me thinking about a spiritual detox, a detox for my inner soul. Some of the letters in the New Testament address and highlight the importance of cleansing our spirit of toxic habits and thoughts that separate us from God. When we allow these attitudes to infiltrate our lives, they can cause exhaustion, disappointment, conflict, and/or discouragement. Just like a physical detox this takes time, planning, commitment, and self-control.

So where do I begin? First, I need to identify the attitudes I want to eliminate or control. Is it anger, selfishness, self-pity, gossip, or impatience? Or could it be one that is listed in 1 Peter or Colossians: deceit, lust, malice, envy, or slander? While I can't see the physical toxins that make me feel sluggish and impatient, it is also difficult to see the attitudes that cause dissatisfaction in my life. It is through a process of self-introspection, meditation, prayer, and reading scripture that the toxins can be identified. However, beware of creating a list of self-deprecating faults that cause discouragement or stress. I wrote my list down, confessed them to the Lord and researched scriptures to help me in my times of weakness. Through this prayer time, I received spiritual insight. The Lord does not want us to focus on the negative, but instead keep our eyes on His promises. I discovered that the way of ridding myself of my toxic attitudes is through confession and keeping my eyes on the Lord. God lovingly and gently calls me to replace negative attitudes with His forgiveness, grace, and love.

If we confess our sins, he is faithful and just and will forgive us our sins and purify us from all unrighteousness, 1 John 1:9.

Devotions for the Distracted Heart

Just as a physical detox renews the energies and health of your body, a spiritual detox can renew a right spirit within you, freeing you to love God and others.

Remember the words from 1 Peter 1:22; *Now that you have purified yourselves by obeying the truth so that you have sincere love for each other love one another deeply, from the heart.* ♥

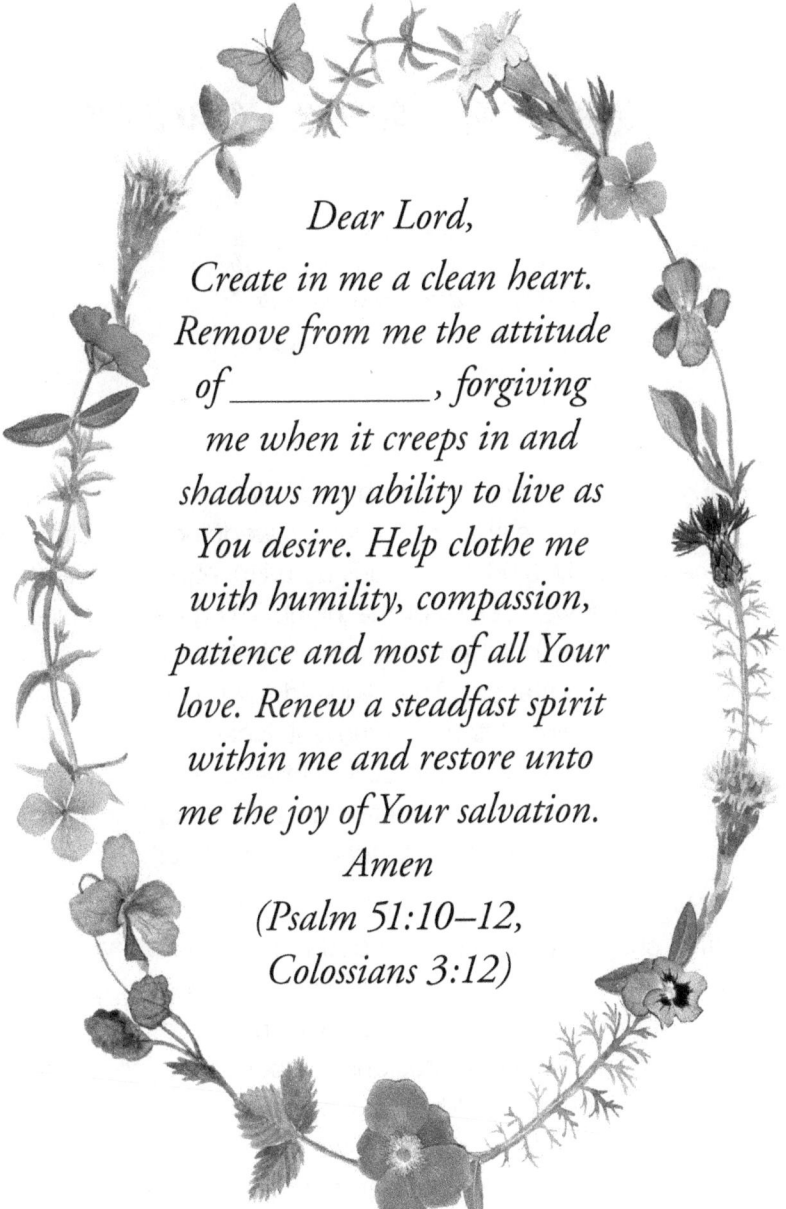

*Dear Lord,
Create in me a clean heart.
Remove from me the attitude
of _____, forgiving
me when it creeps in and
shadows my ability to live as
You desire. Help clothe me
with humility, compassion,
patience and most of all Your
love. Renew a steadfast spirit
within me and restore unto
me the joy of Your salvation.
Amen
(Psalm 51:10–12,
Colossians 3:12)*

Distraction of Delayed Departures

> *We can make our plans, but the Lord determines our steps.*
> —Proverbs 16:9 (NLT)

My husband and I had spent a blessed weekend in Michigan celebrating a family wedding. Our flight home was early, 6:00 a.m., requiring us to leave my sister's house in the wee hours of the night. Things were going smoothly at first, but then I discovered that I had left my cell phone in the rental car. This required my husband to take a time-consuming detour to retrieve it. Needless to say, the frustration was beginning to build. However, having started a bit earlier than planned, there was still time to wait in the long line for that desperately-needed cup of coffee.

After going through security, we finally arrived at the coffee shop. My husband handed me money and went to wait at the gate. As he walked away, the woman behind me complimented my luggage which led to a lengthy conversation and a God-designed appointment. We began sharing with a few worldly exchanges, but God had more in mind. In a matter of seconds, we connected at a deeper level with our faith. We had a lot in common, including how

Distraction of Delayed Departures

God had blessed and used both of us to be His vessels in our separate ministries. We talked quite a while and my new friend, Tara Rayburn, a motivational speaker, ended up inviting me to participate in a live video interview. While I had watched online videos before, this was my first time contributing to one!

I finally returned to my husband and shared my excitement about this new encounter. As I boarded the plane, I couldn't help being amazed with the morning. Just minutes before, I had been stressed and frustrated with my own stupidity, having left the cell phone in the car and retraced steps to retrieve it. It was an unnecessary distraction that caused a delay. This experience made me realize that sometimes God allows distractions to occur for the purpose of causing a delay. Unknown to me, He had a plan, a divine appointment for me, and I would have missed it without the aggravating delay.

Proverbs 16:9 reminds us that *We can make our plans, but the Lord determines our steps.* We had a plan to arrive early to the airport, with time to enjoy coffee together before boarding our plane home. Instead, God wanted to connect me with a Christian sister who lived on the other side of the country. He chose the time, He chose the place, and she had been obedient to His nudge to speak to me.

If God can arrange a divine appointment like this in an airport in Flint, Michigan, think about what He has planned for you! Most of my delays are caused by my own distractions. Sometimes God has a surprise in store with that delay, and sometimes there is a lesson to learn. ♥

Devotions for the Distracted Heart

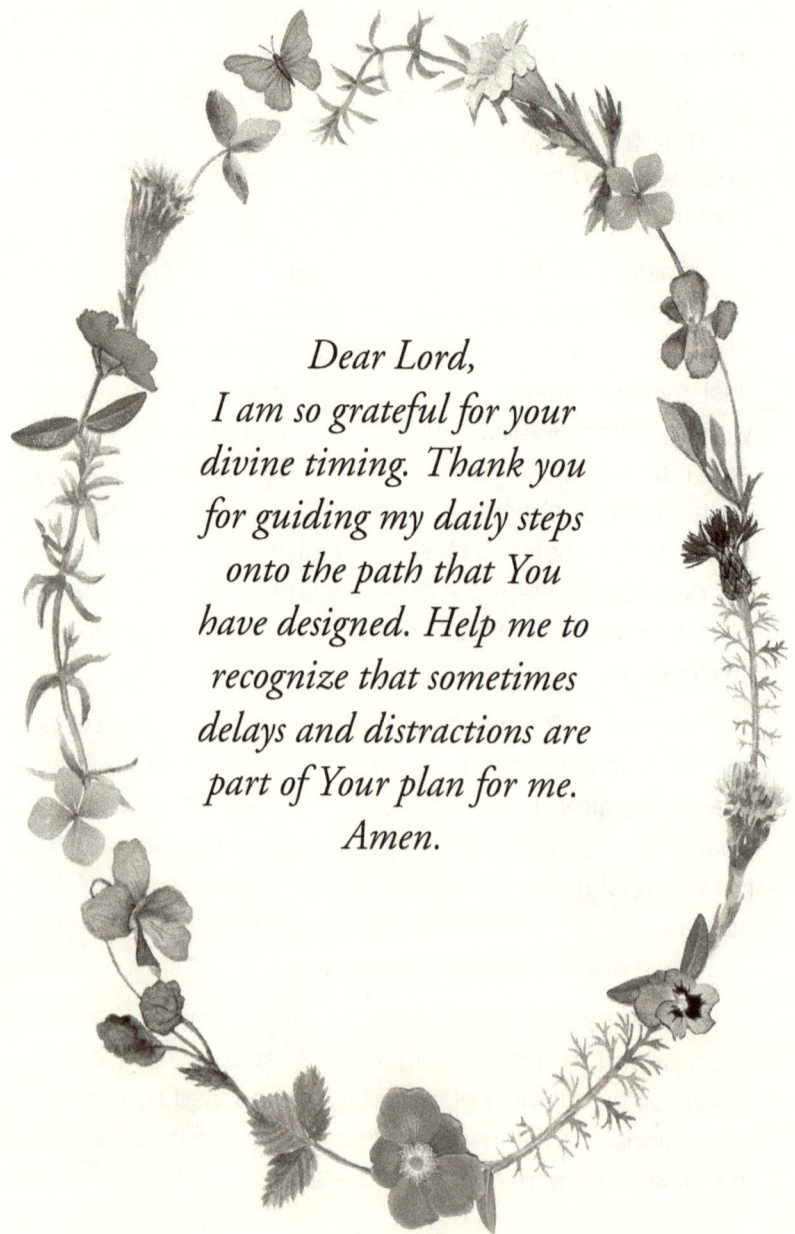

*Dear Lord,
I am so grateful for your divine timing. Thank you for guiding my daily steps onto the path that You have designed. Help me to recognize that sometimes delays and distractions are part of Your plan for me.
Amen.*

Distraction of Diapers

> *Let the little children come to me! Never send them away!*
> *For the Kingdom of God belongs to men who have hearts*
> *as trusting as these little children's…*
> —Luke 18:16 TLB

As I sat down on the couch to do my morning devotion, a goldfish cracker rolled out from behind the pillow. Another reminder of when our grandchildren were living with us. During that time, our house was filled with the sounds and activities of twin two-year-olds. Little things such as snowflakes, light switches, and bugs became events. The house was cluttered with colorful blocks, noisy toys, engaging giggles, sticky finger prints, tired whines, wet kisses, and yes, dirty diapers. These little beings had brought an energy and joy into our lives along with a smile to our souls.

If you have ever cared for toddlers you know the all-encompassing energy this requires. Their schedules and needs become the priority. They require your imaginative energy, constant patience, perpetual care, and continuous love. When you're a grandparent, it is exhausting; when you are a parent, it is all consuming. Nevertheless, when you are caring for these loveable tykes, it's not the messes you dwell on, but the joy in participating in their curious development. No matter how exhausting, it's rewarding to love, comfort, and forgive.

Isn't that like our heavenly Father? He is always loving, slow to anger, and quick to forgive. How many times do we respond to Him like a child? We leave clutter in the way. We get distracted with new toys. We whine when things don't go our way. We don't seek His wisdom first before we worry, cry, or try to hide it. But our Father is patient, understanding, and always compassionate. *As a father has compassion for his children, so the Lord has compassion for those who fear him,* Psalm 103:13.

When the little ones left, the house became eerily quiet with no sounds of *Little Einsteins* or *Mickey Mouse Clubhouse* ringing from the TV. No voices crying out "one more time" or "night, night." We were left with the remnants of fingerprints on the windows, goldfish crackers under the couch, and cherished memories. But the lessons I have learned by looking at life and faith through the eyes of a child, have made a permanent mark on my heart.

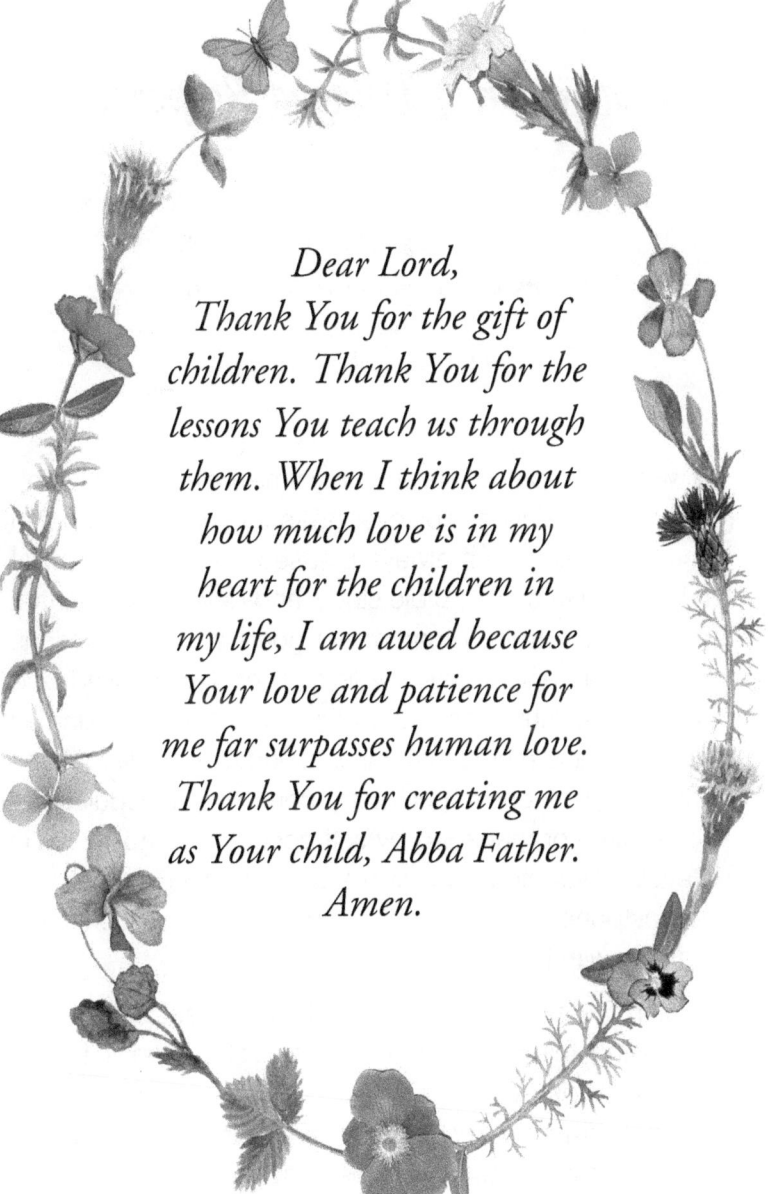

*Dear Lord,
Thank You for the gift of children. Thank You for the lessons You teach us through them. When I think about how much love is in my heart for the children in my life, I am awed because Your love and patience for me far surpasses human love. Thank You for creating me as Your child, Abba Father.
Amen.*

Distraction of Delayed Responses

> *Live a life of love.*
> *Love others just as Christ loved us.*
> —Ephesians 5:2a

I wish I could say I balance my time well every day and prioritize relationships over tasks with no regrets. I wish I could also say I am always pleased with the amount of time I spend in prayer, Bible study, and devotions. But, that is far from the truth. I tend to set goals and expectations for each day and create my lists. Then I'm derailed and distracted by mundane interruptions and activities such as technology and media temptations. Some of the disruptions can be urgent ones, but many could be scheduled for another time or managed by self-control. This ability to be so easily distracted causes me to avoid things on my list and postpone them for another day. Am I the only one who struggles with this?

I don't know about you, but I gain great satisfaction in crossing things off my countless lists. Even if I have to carry things over to a new list, there is still a sense of accomplishment. For years, these lists were filled with tasks to complete, but over time I have realized that I need

Distraction of Delayed Responses

to include connections with those I care about on those lists. Whether it is lunch with a friend, a call, an email, a card, or a walk, including these activities helps me to keep in touch with those I care about. After all, if devotions are on my list, then shouldn't time with family and friends be included as well? Aren't the two greatest commandments, *"to love God with all our heart, mind, soul and strength, and to love our neighbors as ourselves?"* (taken from Luke 10:27) However, I fall into the trap of prioritizing the tasks with calendar deadlines on my lists, while delaying time to spend with loved ones.

    Here is a personal example that occurred. I had intended to reach out to a beautiful sister in Christ that I met many years ago while standing in the line for the restroom in a North Carolina restaurant. It was one of those divine appointments that led to a treasured relationship. Our contacts were few over the years, including cards, calls, and a couple visits. But my life was profoundly touched by this woman who freely witnessed her faith to me and often reached out to encourage me. My most recent communication with her had been in the form of a phone call. I felt the need to reach out to her again, but it was one of those items on my list that I recycled over and over. I am ashamed to admit that this occurred for a couple months. I finally followed through and sent a note apologizing for my delay and included several pictures to update her on what was happening in my life. A few weeks later, a response I did not anticipate arrived. It was a card from North Carolina, but the handwriting was not my friend's. Her daughter graciously and lovingly took time to write me to let me know that her Mom had gone to be with the Lord, six weeks before I sent my card.

This hit me right in the heart. How could I have let my daily distractions delay such a simple thing as a card, or a phone call or even an email? I am grateful her daughter, in her grief, reached out to me, but I was convicted with guilt because of my own delay. I immediately wrote a card expressing my sympathy for her loss, including my appreciation for her taking the time to write, and my great respect for her mom, I found myself grieving the loss of this very special woman and dealing with my own personal regrets.

Thomas Jefferson wisely stated, "Never put off till tomorrow what you can do today." I believe this quote holds value and I need to remember this every day. If I am going to live by the two greatest commandments, I need to focus on behaviors that demonstrate my love for God and for others, not put them off until tomorrow. Will I choose to use my time each day to model this priority, or will I allow those mundane distractions to cause delays that lead to regret? Will I listen and follow through with the nudging of the Holy Spirit? ♥

Distraction of Delayed Responses

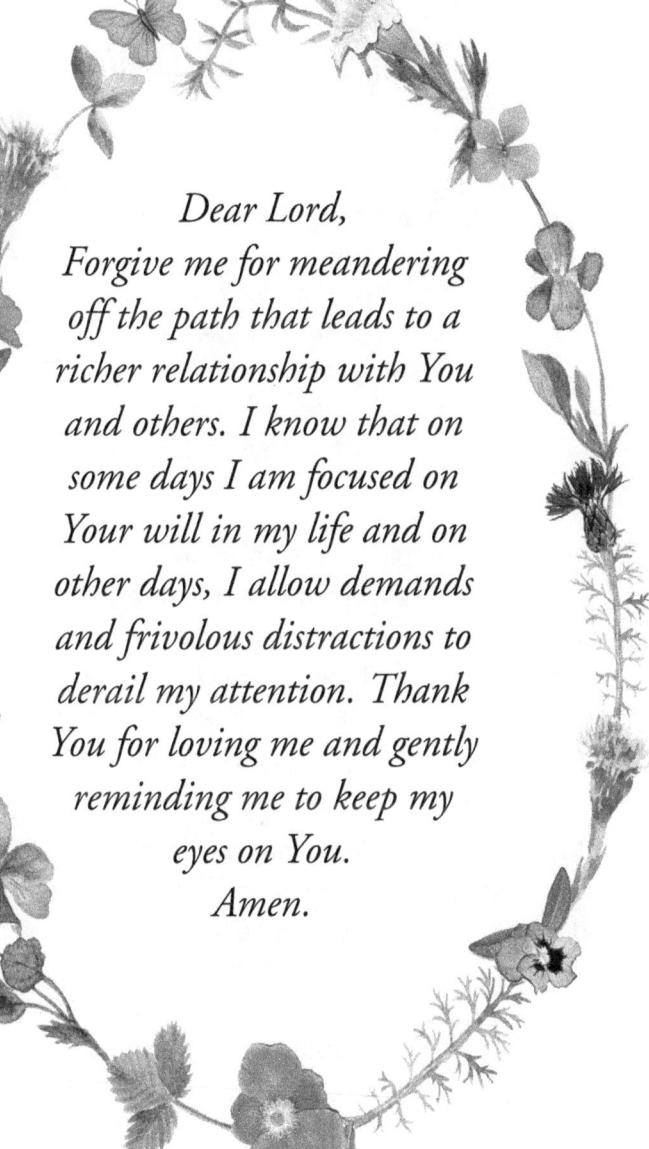

*Dear Lord,
Forgive me for meandering off the path that leads to a richer relationship with You and others. I know that on some days I am focused on Your will in my life and on other days, I allow demands and frivolous distractions to derail my attention. Thank You for loving me and gently reminding me to keep my eyes on You.
Amen.*

Distraction of Denim

> *And why do you worry about clothes? See how the flowers of the field grow. They do not labor or spin. Yet I tell you that not even Solomon in all his splendor was dressed like one of these. If that is how God clothes the grass of the field, which is here today and tomorrow is thrown into the fire, will he not much more clothe you—you of little faith?*
> —Matthew 6:28–30

As a little girl I remember my Dad calling jeans, "dungarees," which he only wore as work pants for physical chores. Then denim began to grace the fashion scene. Instead of it being used only for manual labor uniforms, designers started marketing name-brand fashion jeans for everyone, eventually expanding to jackets, jumpers, skirts, and more.

My first job in college was working as a file clerk in a business office. I thought it was an important job since it had a title. It was a typical secretarial pool setting much like the ones in movies where there is a big room lined with desks and women typing at their desks. The office was filled with cliquish and catty women and I was the outsider. I was never included in conversations or invited to sit with them at lunch. I felt like I was back in middle school. It didn't help to have a controlling manager who did what she could to over-power and intimidate me. I did my best to follow the rules and complete each task to exceed her expectations, but nothing was ever appreciated or recognized. I tried dressing up to be more business-like, since many of the women came in shapeless tops and the type of polyester slacks my mother would wear for chores.

One day, I walked into work wearing my interview outfit: a navy blazer, collared tucked-in shirt, light blue denim, pleated, cuffed pants, and chunky heeled boots. I thought I looked pretty sharp. However, first thing in the morning, the manager came over to me and reamed me out in front of all the other women for wearing shabby denim to work. She told me it was inappropriate and if I wore it again, I would lose my job because it was against the dress code to wear "tacky" jeans. Her comments stung me like bullets with judgment and intimidation. I was humiliated and wanted to quit but survived the day. Today, you see jeans in almost every fashion setting. It appears that the stigma around denim no longer exists, and work places even have a "dress-down" Friday where they allow jeans.

After this incident, I became aware that what we wear each day can have a big impact on our image and attitude. Some of us worry about what we are going to wear, what is appropriate for the situation, what are the expectations for the event, and what outfit will help us feel the best. We try to make sure we do not stick out as too dressy or casual. We can be encouraged with a compliment but equally devastated with a negative comment. Putting such a high priority on our outer appearance can distract us from our purpose, mission, and consequently alter our inner spirit.

Jesus warns us about this in his Sermon on the Mount, *"And why do you worry about clothes? See how the flowers of the field grow. They do not labor or spin. Yet I tell you that not even Solomon in all his splendor was dressed like one of these. If that is how God clothes the grass of the field, which is here today and tomorrow is thrown into the fire, will he not much more clothe you—you of little faith?"* Matthew 6: 28–30.

This scripture is challenging us to trust God and depend on Him for all of our needs. Sure, it's fun to collect shoes, dress in stylish colors and fabrics, but if it consumes our focus, then it weakens our spirit rather than strengthens our witness. So what does God want us to do? Paul gives an answer, *"We are called to clothe ourselves with compassion, kindness, humility, gentleness and patience. Bear with each other and forgive one another if any of us has a grievance against someone. Forgive as the Lord forgave you. And over all these virtues put on love, which binds them all together in perfect unity,* Colossians 3:12b–14. I think this is what Jesus meant in the Sermon on the Mount. He does not want us to worry about our clothing or physical appearance. He promises to meet all our needs if we look to Him. His desire is for us to focus on our inner spirit.

So the next time you go to your closet to choose the outfit for an occasion, don't be distracted by the style, fabric, or the fit. Instead spend more time clothing yourself with compassion, kindness, humility, gentleness, patience, and above all else, clothe yourself in love for that is what ties everything together in perfect unity! ♥

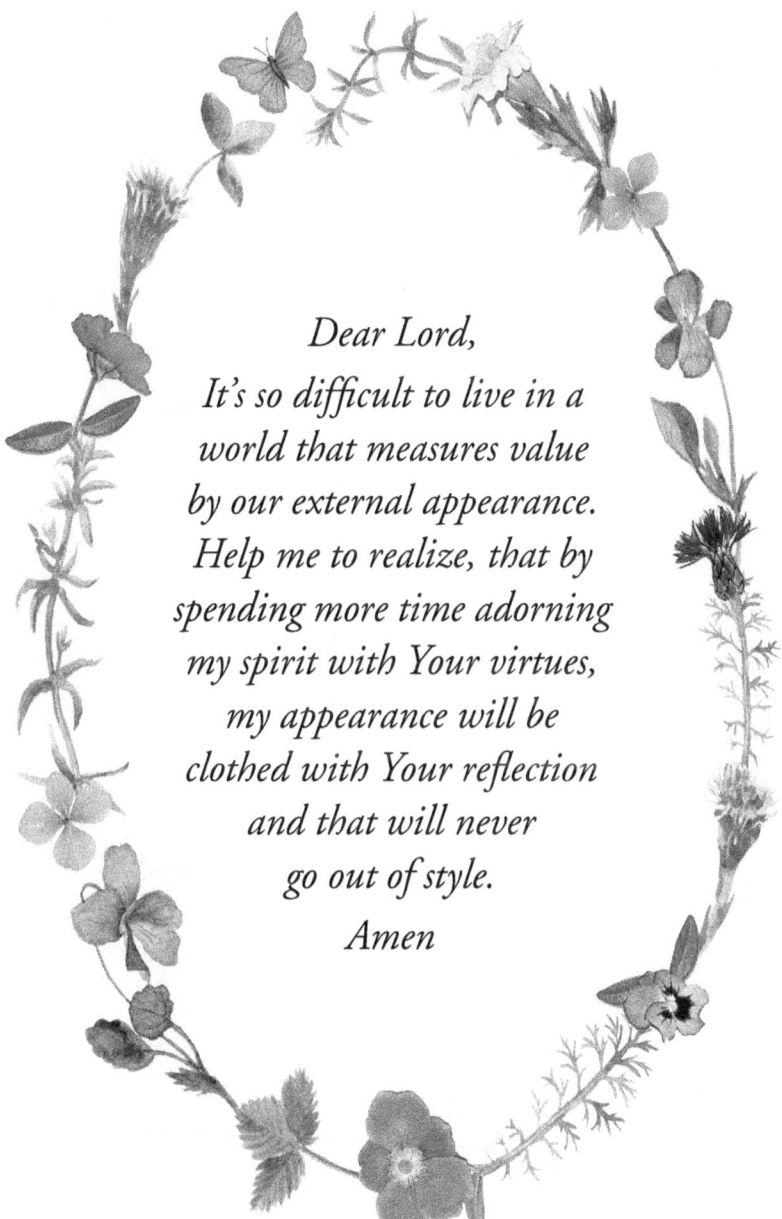

*Dear Lord,
It's so difficult to live in a world that measures value by our external appearance. Help me to realize, that by spending more time adorning my spirit with Your virtues, my appearance will be clothed with Your reflection and that will never go out of style.
Amen*

Distraction of Disappointment

> *We can rejoice, too, when we run into problems and trials, for we know that they help us develop endurance. And endurance develops strength of character, and character strengthens our confident hope of salvation. And this hope will not lead to disappointment. For we know how dearly God loves us, because he has given us the Holy Spirit to fill our hearts with his love.*
> —Romans 5:3–5 New Living Translation (NLT)

Donned in my favorite birthday outfit, candy-striped peddle-pushers with a pink-speckled, mohair sweater, I took one last look at myself in the mirror. "This is the day I have been waiting for!" You see, I was nine years old, and I could now attend the junior choir practice at church. I wanted to look as grown up as I could! Ever since first grade, I had longed to wear one of those royal blue robes, sit in the special seats in the front of the sanctuary, and actually sing for the church. I loved music and could hear the group practice each week. By the time they performed the song in church, I was humming right along with the group! I had already sung a solo for the mother-daughter banquet in the second grade, thus I thought I was ready.

Today was my first practice! My stomach was doing somersaults as I skipped up the sidewalk to the church entrance, opened the heavy front door, and stepped into the dark vestibule. The building was eerily quiet, and as I neared the sanctuary, my excitement turned to nervous fear. I opened the door and saw the choir gathered at the front of the church. My legs felt like jelly as I walked down the long center aisle towards the group. *What will I say? Will they greet me? Where will I sit? What if they think I am a baby?"*

I mustered all the confidence I could on the outside, knowing there was nothing but mush on the inside, and boldly approached the choir. Mrs. Johnson, the director, spotted me and called out in front of everyone, "Well, what are you doing here?"

I swallowed hard and answered timidly, "I just turned nine and—"

"Nine?" she bellowed. "This choir is only open to 4th graders and older. You are welcome to join us next September."

I wanted to speak up and remind Mrs. Johnson she had told my mom I could join after my ninth birthday, but every eye was on me and the snickers added to my humiliation. Without a word, I ran down the aisle, through the dark hall, and out of the church. As I pushed through the front door out into the cold, tears stung my eyes, and my throat choked with sobs. "Why did this happen?"

The short walk home seemed like an eternity. I didn't dare go inside and tell my family what happened. They would be so disappointed in me. Instead, I sat on my favorite garden brick wall and cried until there were no tears left.

As a child, this experience permeated my spirit and defeated my confidence. Even as I write this, I can still feel the sting, yet it pales in comparison to so many challenges I've had in my life since that day. Even as a child, I questioned why God allowed this to happen. Why does He allow us to experience disappointments, difficulties, and defeats?

We can rejoice, too, when we run into problems and trials, for we know that they help us develop endurance. And endurance develops strength of character, and character strengthens our confident hope of salvation. And this hope will not lead to disappointment. For we know how dearly God loves us, because he has given us the Holy Spirit to fill our hearts with his love, Romans 5:3–5. (NLT)

Little did I know as a young girl I would experience many disappointments throughout my life. As the above scripture says, trials strengthen us and develop our character. It is through hope that God fills our hearts with His love. Even Mrs. Johnson softened. I think my mom probably spoke with her, and she finally relented to let me join the choir for the Easter season later that same year.

This disappointment does not hold a candle to the deep concerns you may be dealing with, but I know that we have a loving God who is reaching out to you in your trials. He holds you and wipes the tears from your eyes in those times of desperation. When you present your concerns to Him you may be in a time of character building, but remember you are not alone. He is there loving, caring, strengthening, and holding you. ♥

The Distraction of Disappointment

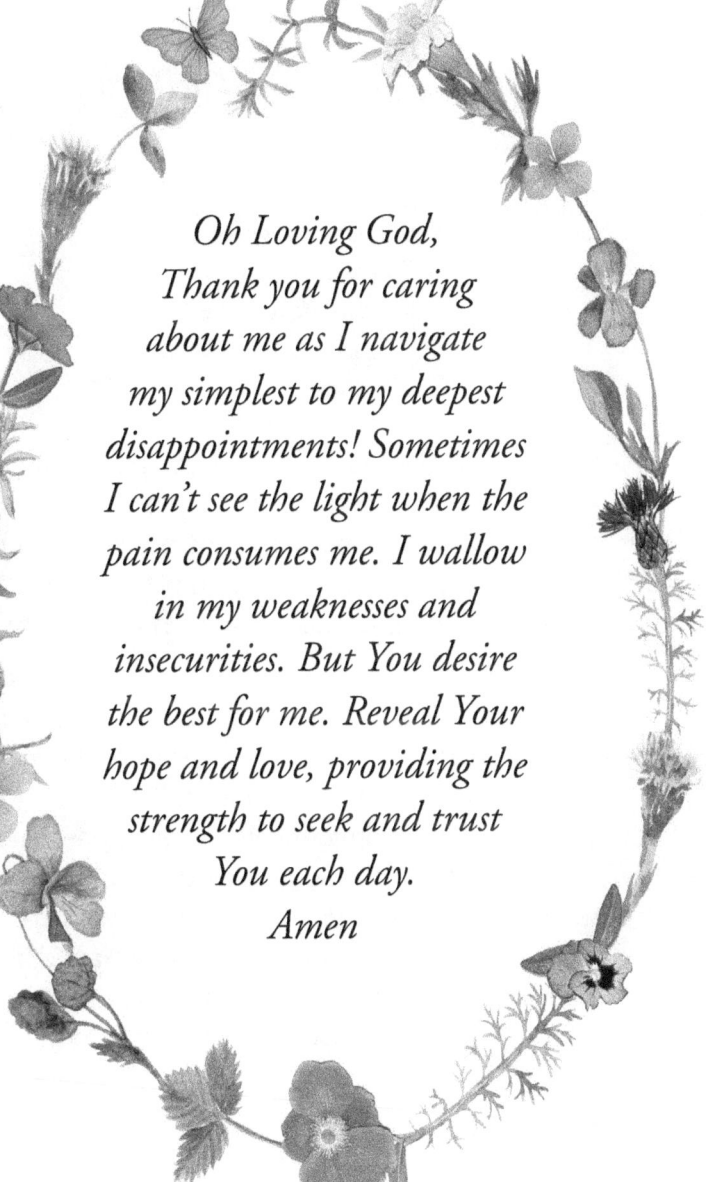

*Oh Loving God,
Thank you for caring
about me as I navigate
my simplest to my deepest
disappointments! Sometimes
I can't see the light when the
pain consumes me. I wallow
in my weaknesses and
insecurities. But You desire
the best for me. Reveal Your
hope and love, providing the
strength to seek and trust
You each day.
Amen*

Distraction of Decluttering

> *Do not store up for yourselves treasures on earth...*
> —Matthew 6:19a

Keep it simple, less is more, and don't sweat the small stuff are familiar phrases referring to ways we clutter our lives. This includes not only tangible items, but also activities, expectations, and even emotions. Decluttering and downsizing are processes that help us simplify each of these areas.

Over the past years, I have cleaned out several family homes only to return to my own and feel the need to declutter. I realize I hold on to more "STUFF" than I need. Yet, making the decision to throw something away is very difficult. I know it's healthier to discard items than to keep and store them for a rainy day, but there is always that "what if" voice in the back of my head. Other items are difficult to give away because they represent special memories or an emotional connection to someone important to me. It's all so overwhelming!

The process of decluttering may be simple to describe, but if you are like me, it is not easy to implement. I marvel

The Distraction of Decluttering

at my adult children and the ways they are able to make decisions to keep their clutter to a minimum. For me it is not that simple. I don't think it's the decluttering that is the distraction, but it's the stress in deciding what to do with the clutter.

I have several friends who help people organize, declutter, and simplify their surroundings. They each have a critical yet compassionate eye to support others in making difficult decisions. The typical categories for decluttering are discard, donate, or keep. There are specific questions that guide this process: Have I used this item in the last year? If no, follow up with; Does it have the potential to find purpose in someone else's life? If yes, donate it. If no, discard it.

For the special things that are filled with memories, the questions and process are a bit different. Does it add joy to my life? If so, does it need to be saved, or could I take a picture, write down my personal recollections, and save them in a scrapbook? To say the least, this process takes up a lot less space than the items themselves. Better yet, I could make a digital file and store it on my computer–no clutter at all! Truth be told, I haven't embraced this practice yet, but perhaps over the next months, I will be able to do so. For the treasured items that bring me joy, I need to find a practical way to either display them or organize them in an orderly and logical manner with boxes and labels.

Over the past two months, I have been doing my best to implement this process. It has empowered me to discard, sell, and donate several carloads of household items and numerous boxes of collectables and treasures. I am making progress; however, I feel like I have not made a dent in the looming task ahead.

Jesus reminds us in the Sermon on the Mount not to place too much value on our earthly treasures.

"Do not store up for yourselves treasures on earth, where moths and vermin destroy, and where thieves break in and steal. But store up for yourselves treasures in heaven, where moths and vermin do not destroy, and where thieves do not break in and steal. For where your treasure is, there your heart will be also." Matthew 6:19–21

Are there areas of your life that are cluttered and need some attention? Are you storing up treasures on earth or in heaven? ♱

The Distraction of Decluttering

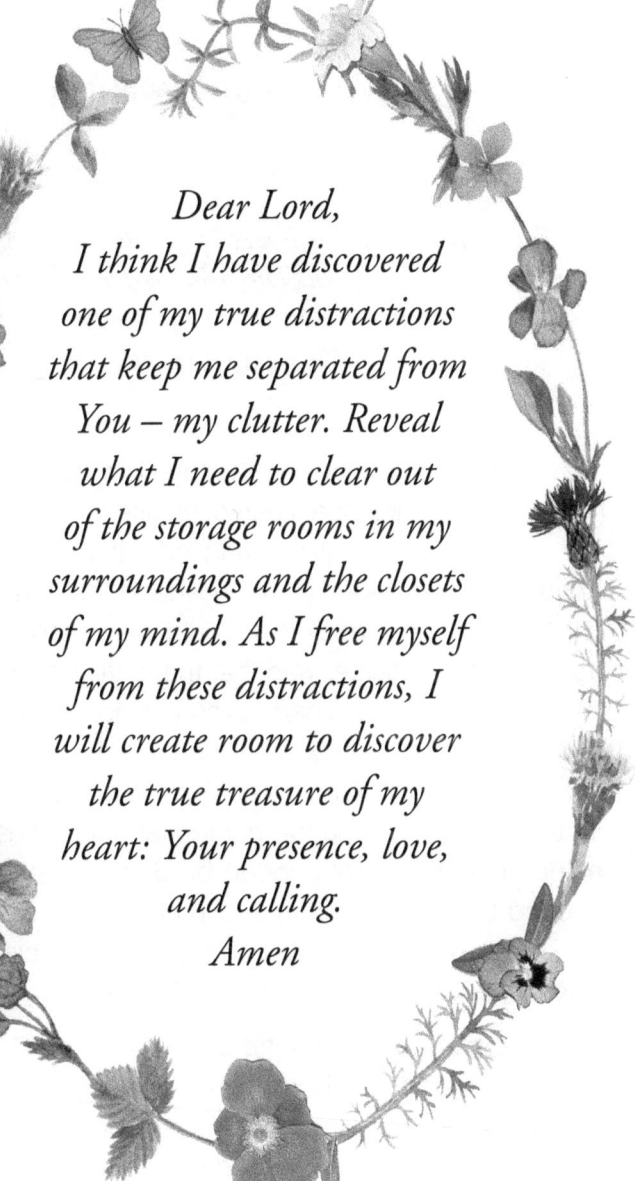

*Dear Lord,
I think I have discovered
one of my true distractions
that keep me separated from
You — my clutter. Reveal
what I need to clear out
of the storage rooms in my
surroundings and the closets
of my mind. As I free myself
from these distractions, I
will create room to discover
the true treasure of my
heart: Your presence, love,
and calling.
Amen*

Distraction of Diamonds

> *The Lord their God will save his people on that day as a shepherd saves his flock. They will sparkle in his land like jewels in a crown. How attractive and beautiful they will be!*
> —Zechariah 9:16–17a

I have to admit, I love pretty, sparkly, things. I have been known to purchase a purse, blouse, or piece of jewelry just because of the glimmering adornments added to it. I had a running joke with my husband that if my birthday gift fit in his coat pocket, I would be a happy wife. My assumption of course, was that the small box would have jewelry in it. He always had fun surprising me with little gifts and sometimes the box contained a note sending me on a scavenger hunt. Other times he presented me with an ornament or small change purse that actually had jewelry hidden in it. It did not need to be diamond jewelry. It just needed to be shimmering and pretty to make me happy. If it contained a diamond, it was an extra special surprise! After all, diamonds are a girl's best friend. Or are they?

The symbol of a diamond is one of beauty, value, and eternity. Diamonds add splendor to many elegant pieces of jewelry because of their ability to refract light, bringing brilliance to the piece. They are a valuable and desired gem, so much so that there are many laboratories striving to replicate stones with the same qualities as a diamond. They are the hardest of the precious gems, giving them the ability to last forever. Because of these characteristics, diamond engagement rings are commonly given as an outward symbol of the spiritual commitment in a marriage covenant.

But a diamond was not always beautiful. It is actually formed from carbon, a black chalky mineral found in volcanic magma. Only after millions of years, with high temperatures and extreme pressure can the carbon atoms align to form the tetrahedron crystals found in a beautiful, luminous diamond. In essence, because of an excruciating process, beauty is created from ashes.

Isn't this what Jesus Christ does for us when He comes into our lives? He takes our broken, charred pieces and aligns them to make them whole. He takes our colorless spirit and shines His light through us to reflect His love. The process of this Christ-like change is not instantaneous. Just like a diamond, our spiritual walk is transformed through the pressures of the world and the heat of adversities. Keeping our eyes on the light of the Holy Spirit helps us align our will with His so that we will shine like diamonds in His world. In The Message translation, Zechariah 9:16–17a says, *"Their God will rescue them and they will become like gemstones in a crown, catching all the colors of the sun. Then how they will shine, shimmer, and glow!"*

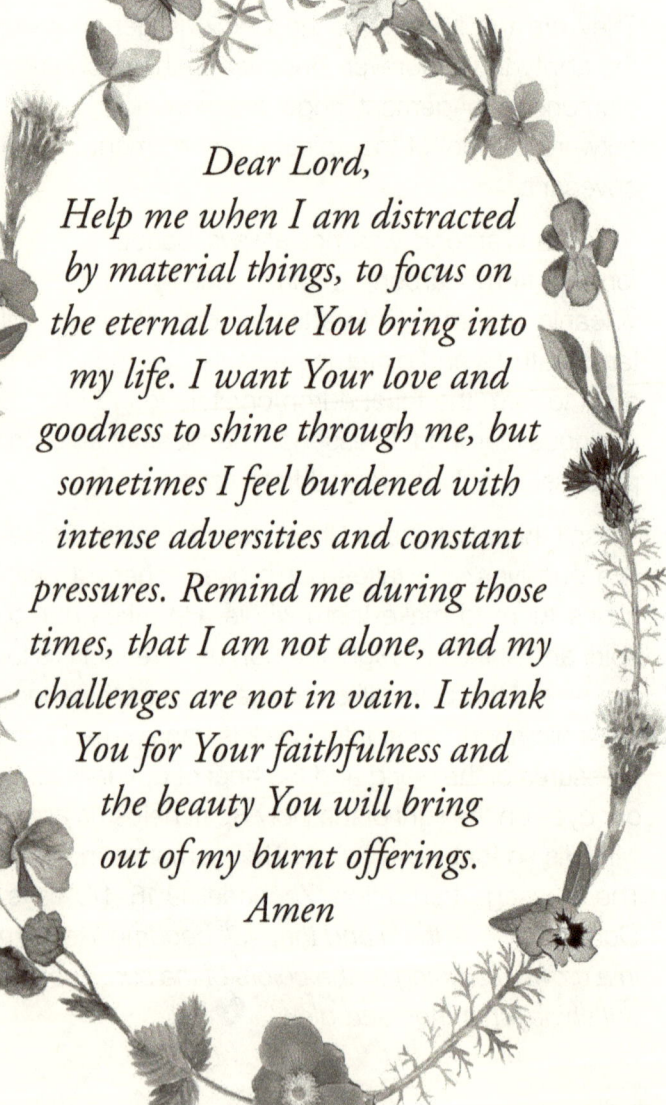

*Dear Lord,
Help me when I am distracted by material things, to focus on the eternal value You bring into my life. I want Your love and goodness to shine through me, but sometimes I feel burdened with intense adversities and constant pressures. Remind me during those times, that I am not alone, and my challenges are not in vain. I thank You for Your faithfulness and the beauty You will bring out of my burnt offerings.
Amen*

Distraction of Departures from the Familiar

> *Be strong and courageous, for you must go with this people into the land that the Lord swore to their ancestors to give them, and you must divide it among them as their inheritance. The Lord himself goes before you and will be with you; he will never leave you nor forsake you. Do not be afraid; do not be discouraged.*
> —Deuteronomy 31:7b–8

Departures can be exciting as you might be preparing for a once in a lifetime vacation, or you may be returning to that favorite spot where you connect with family, friends, or God. However, there is much to organize before you leave, and these tasks can consume your time and thoughts.

Several years ago, I watched as my each of my children independently prepared for more permanent departures; the departure of relocation. Both are married with families and at different times, stepped out in faith like their fore fathers Moses and Abraham, to relocate in a new state. It has involved great courage as my son, daughter, and their spouses have taken on different jobs, while simultaneously setting up new homes.

I began to question my own trust level when God called my husband and me to step out in faith and follow them across the country. I had lived in the same house for over thirty years, and worked at the same job for more than fifteen. There was comfort in my routine and life. I had roots in this area and deep relationships that had nurtured, supported, and encouraged me to grow. Now God had other plans and my faith was about to be tested on a whole new level.

It was exciting, nerve-wracking, challenging, and difficult all at the same time! The process was bittersweet as we said good-bye to many dear friends who had become like family. In addition, we sold a house full of memories to establish a new home for a different season!

As we left our home on that final day, my husband and I held each other and sobbed in the empty family room. The memories in that home will forever be imprinted in our spirits and minds. After we composed ourselves, we prayed. We thanked God for the blessings and the memories of the home, and prayed for the new family moving in that day. Then, we took a final picture. In God's providence, He blessed us with a spiritual visitation that could be seen in the photograph as a white cloud in the shape of a man.

To understand the significance of this image, I need to share with you a bit of history. Right before my father departed from this world, he spoke of seeing family members "not in their skin." We all have different beliefs on the visitation of angels and spirits, but I believe that God knew I needed a tangible confirmation from Him as we departed from a treasured and predictable life, for a new adventure.

Distraction of Departures from the Familiar

Departures can be frightening, devastating, or exciting. Remember, just as Joshua took over Moses leadership, in the journey to the Promised Land, *The Lord himself goes before you and will be with you; he will never leave you nor forsake you. Do not be afraid; do not be discouraged,* Deuteronomy 31:8.

Are you experiencing the loss of a departed loved one or a pending departure? No matter what season you are in, it is my prayer that you can feel the peace and strength of God through the process and be grateful. You are never alone. ♥

Dear Lord, It is so easy to stay comfortable in my familiar routines and surroundings. I say yes to the predictable but often respond with hesitation when you lead me in a new direction. You are paving the path for me providing courage to travel in new directions as needed. Comfort me when the new direction involves a loss. Thank you for Your divine guidance and patience when I question you. To You be Glory and Honor! Amen

Distraction of Dessert

> *Taste and see that the Lord is good;*
> —Psalm 34:8a

Cheesecake, ice cream, pies, and mousse are just a few of the delectable delights that can turn my head and tempt me into consuming more calories than my stomach can handle. Have you noticed how restaurants will tempt you into partaking of these desserts? Typically a server will discuss the appetizer and main dish specials with you when ordering. Then after they clear all the plates from the table, they give you some time to sit and talk while a tray of beautifully displayed sweet indulgences is brought to your table.

It's as if the entire meal was a preparation for the dessert at the end. I find that many times my eyes are bigger than my stomach. I can eat everything during the meal, yet still want to finish with a delectable delight, only to complain afterwards because I ate too much. To avoid this dilemma, I have a friend who made a practice of ordering dessert first! She always planned to enjoy the sweetest taste sensations before she ate the rest of her meal. Thus she would never miss dessert because of eating too much during the meal.

Distraction of Dessert

Have you ever thought of dessert as a parallel to heaven? We hear about heaven in sermons, and artists and playwrights produce creative imagery of it. We have accounts from people who have experienced after-death encounter. Many describe enticing, warm, and loving stories about their encounters with the true dessert of life. Heaven, is it the delectable delight at the end of a faithful life?

If we use this analogy, then are our lives the main course and heaven the sweet indulgence at the end? Does this mean over indulging in this life on gluttonous temptations, would impact our prospect of eternity with God?

Christ said, *"I am the Way, the Truth and the Life. No one comes to the Father except through me,"* John 14:6. Without a conscious choice to accept Christ, we do not receive the promise of heaven. A right relationship with the Father is the essential step we must take in this main course of life to ensure the possibility of heaven.

It is easy to live an unbridled life that indulges in every enjoyable temptation available. There are many warnings throughout the scriptures that caution us of the destruction this produces. Proverbs is full of them, and Galatians also addresses many of the struggles we encounter between the flesh and the Spirit. *Whoever sows to please their flesh, from the flesh will reap destruction; whoever sows to please the Spirit, from the Spirit will reap eternal life,* Galatians 6:8. Just as we must discipline ourselves during a meal to have room for dessert, so we must discipline our lives to reap the benefit of heaven.

Devotions for the Distracted Heart

And what about my friend who wanted dessert before the meal? Jesus tried to explain in earthly terms what the kingdom of heaven was like. Maybe having dessert before a meal is one way to experience heaven on earth. No matter how you imagine heaven, remember it is only a glimpse and will never compare to the sweet indulgence that God promises to those who are His.

 Heaven, is it the delectable delight at the end of a faithful life?

Distraction of Dessert

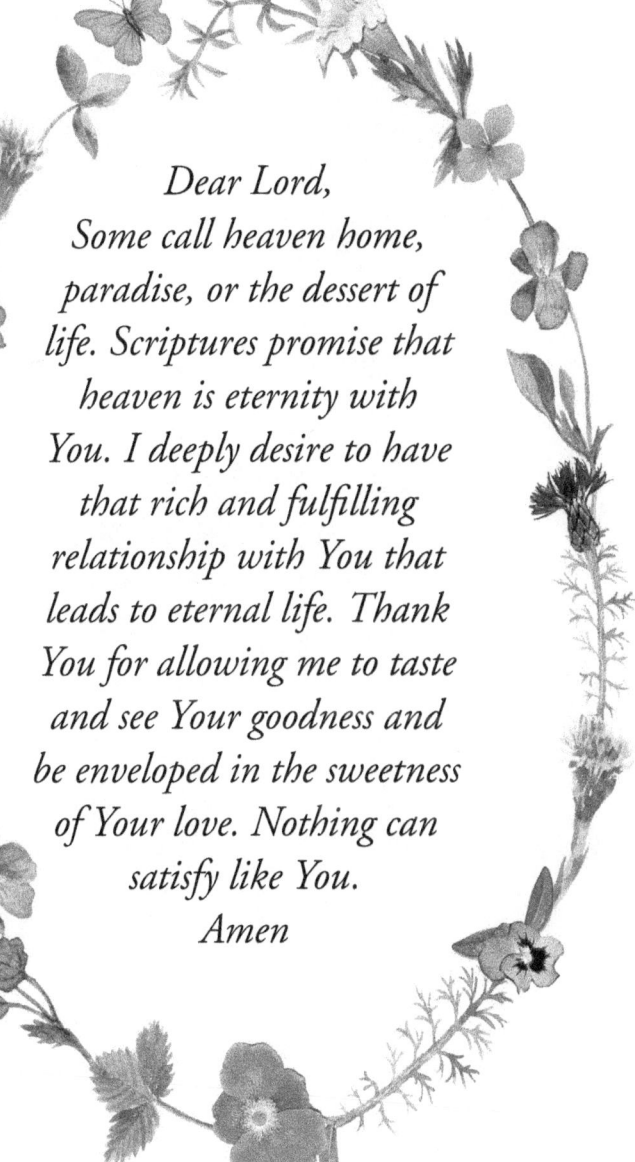

Dear Lord,
Some call heaven home, paradise, or the dessert of life. Scriptures promise that heaven is eternity with You. I deeply desire to have that rich and fulfilling relationship with You that leads to eternal life. Thank You for allowing me to taste and see Your goodness and be enveloped in the sweetness of Your love. Nothing can satisfy like You.
Amen

Distraction of Doors

> *Here I am! I stand at the door and knock. If anyone hears my voice and opens the door, I will come in and eat with that person, and they with me.*
> —Revelation 3:20

"What's behind Door #2?" was a common phrase heard on the old game show, "Let's Make a Deal". In this show, the contestant was given three doors from which to choose. Behind two were desirable prizes and behind one was a "zonk"- something useless. After the contestant chose a door, before opening it, the host began trying to entice her to reconsider her choice. Sometimes he revealed a wonderful prize behind an alternate door or offered a tempting, tangible cash prize in lieu of the one she selected. Tension built as contestants struggled with whether to take the attractive offer or wait for the unknown selection which could be better, or worse.

Thinking about this made me realize that my choices sometimes resemble the "Let's Make a Deal" process. With several possibilities in front of me, I can be swayed by the temptation of an immediate reward. Of course, it is more desirable to know all the facts and potential consequences of choices before making a decision, but this is not possible.

The Distraction of Doors

It takes courage, tenacity, and faith in God's plan to wait for the unknown. I often forget that He does not want to "zonk" me. He desires far better things than I could ever imagine. *For I have plans for you says the Lord. Plans to prosper and not to harm you. Plans to give you a hope and a future,* Jeremiah 29:11.

The phrase, "When God closes a door, He opens a window," is a reminder that He not only knows the plan, He has an alternative path when it appears that I have taken a detour. My view is often narrow, and in the midst of my own disappointments and challenges, I can't see all the possibilities. I don't even have the energy to consider what alternatives God might have behind doors #2 or #3. I am tempted to be satisfied and restricted to my visible circumstances. But God calls me *to live by faith, not by sight,* 2 Corinthians 5:7. I not only need to trust God in His infinite wisdom, I need to exercise patience when His plan doesn't match my expectations. *But if I hope for what I do not yet have, I wait for it patiently,* Romans 8:25.

Are you distracted or overwhelmed by the possible doors that you might choose to open and step through? Listen for the knock of the Savior. He is behind one of them, waiting, ready to take you down a road less travelled, a road of hope.

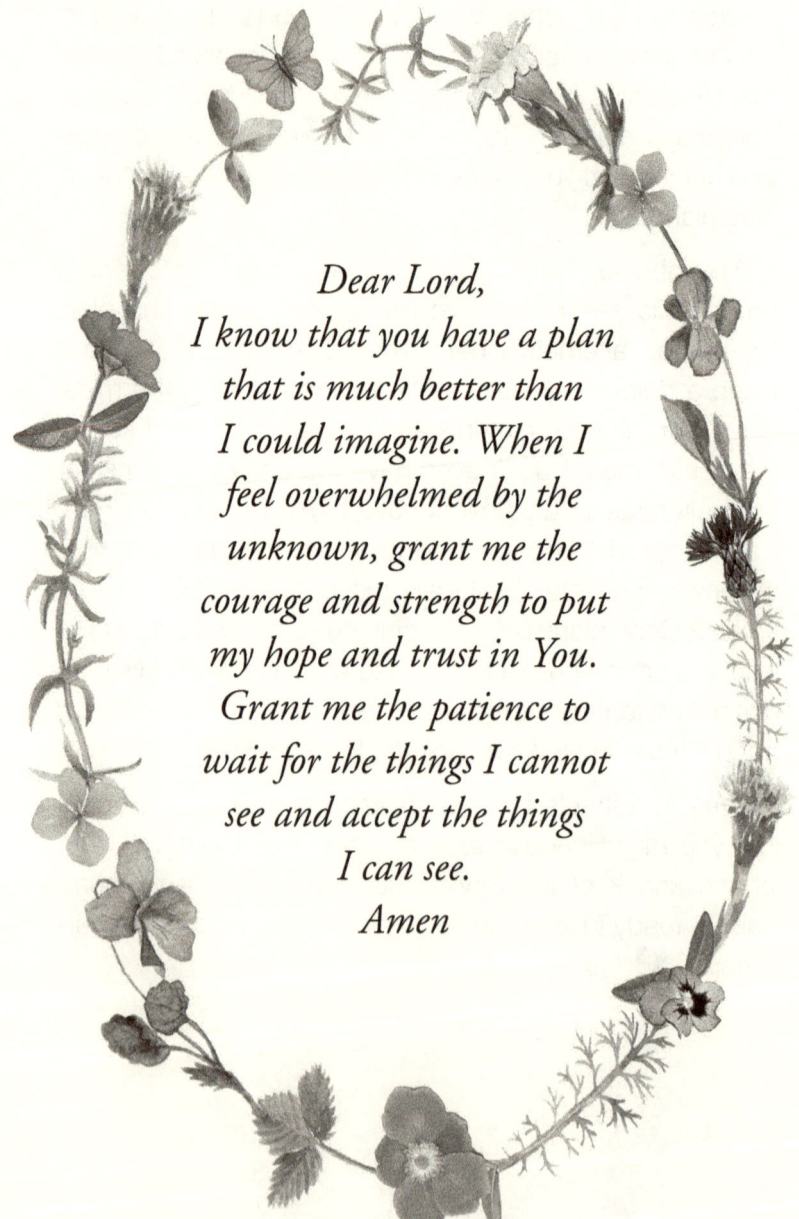

*Dear Lord,
I know that you have a plan
that is much better than
I could imagine. When I
feel overwhelmed by the
unknown, grant me the
courage and strength to put
my hope and trust in You.
Grant me the patience to
wait for the things I cannot
see and accept the things
I can see.
Amen*

Distraction of Departures

> *The Lord himself goes before you and will be with you; he will never leave you nor forsake you. Do not be afraid; do not be discouraged.*
>
> —Deuteronomy 31:8

While standing in the Flint airport security line, my mind was flooded with memories. I thought about how many times I had waited in these security lines in anticipation of a vacation to an exciting destination or a long awaited visit with family or friends. When I began this trip, I had left my home in Maryland and travelled to California with my husband to celebrate his brother's wedding. After the family festivities had concluded, a phone call caused me to quickly change my departing flight from California. Instead of boarding the plane for home, I was soon on my way to Michigan, fearing it might be the last days with my father.

After 15 days in Michigan, I was preparing to return home. But this departure was unlike any I had experienced in the past For years I had been flying to Michigan to visit my dad and I savored the sweet moments we had together. Now I stood in the security line tugging a small suitcase packed with a few of his cherished items, feeling like an orphan and wondering if the airport agent could read my troubled thoughts as he checked my ID and stamped my ticket.

I aimlessly placed my shoes, jacket, purse, and suitcase on the moving belt and trudged through the x-ray booth. When I reached the other side, the TSA agent asked me to step aside while they inspected my suitcase. This caught me completely off guard. For these men, this was a standard procedure, but for me, at that moment, it seemed like a personal violation. I stood there, helplessly watching them rummage through my carefully packed cherished items. My eyes welled up and tears rolled down my cheeks. I felt they were desecrating something very precious to me. When they were through, they simply handed me the disassembled bag and returned to their job.

The tears continued to flow as I repacked each heirloom and attempted to walk to my gate. I was sure every eye was on me, watching my weeping turn into uncontrollable sobs. I darted into the nearest women's bathroom, locked myself in a stall, and blubbered like a baby. My spirit was filled with grief, my precious things were violated, and the world was continuing on as if nothing had happened. I called my brother and sister-in-law for comfort. They listened to my woes and reminded me that this would not be the last time I would feel like this. When a loved one departs, the path of grief is paved with many bumps, ruts, and pot holes. This was my first pot hole.

When Joshua was departing with the Israelites to cross the Jordan, Moses reminded him that *"The Lord himself goes before you and will be with you; he will never leave you nor forsake you. Do not be afraid; do not be discouraged."*

Distraction of Departures

Deuteronomy 31:8. Whether we are departing for a new location, business, family visits, or leaving a loved one, we are never alone. The Lord is not only with us, He goes before us. He prepares the path and travels with us. Sometimes we are not aware of His presence, but He is there.

I eventually gathered myself together in that bathroom stall and made my way to the gate. This trip began with a departure from home to California for an exciting family event, followed by a departure from California to see my dad as he departed from this life to his heavenly home. In each of my departures, I left something familiar, but now I was headed into a new stage in life. Although unfamiliar, I can hear my dad's voice reminding me that "the Lord goes before me". ♥

Dear Lord, Many times I would rather remain in familiar territory, but You call me to leave comfortable places to step into new adventures. Help me remember that each stage of life brings new challenges. I am so grateful for Your words of encouragement when You remind me; When I am weak, You are strong. When I am afraid, You remind me of Your promises. Thank You Lord, for being there in my comings and goings each day. Amen.

Distraction of Detours

> *Fear not, I am with you, be not dismayed, for I am your God. I will strengthen you, help you and uphold you by my righteous right hand.*
> —Isaiah 41:10

One night, on our way out to dinner, my husband took a new route, putting us on a convoluted detour. Rush hour traffic further delayed our scheduled arrival time which increased the anxiety between us. As he turned back onto the familiar route, the sight of the moon hovering on the horizon caused us to draw in a breath. It was at least ten times its normal size. We pulled to the side of the road as we were both mesmerized with a gift we would not have experienced without the detour.

There are many types of detours we experience in life. Some reroute our path while we're traveling. Then there are those that interrupt our lives and deviate our route in directions we had not planned to journey. Sometimes we end up on a detour because we have made the wrong turn. Sometimes it is the result of circumstances out of our control. Each detour has its own set of challenges and can increase our anxiety as we travel unknown paths with unexpected twists and turns. Sometimes it is filled with ruts

Distraction of Detours

and bumps that cause pain, or increase our distress as we fear that we will never return to the path of familiarity and strength.

In Isaiah, God promises that we are not to fear or become dismayed at any time in our life. He reassures us that we are never alone; He is with us. He comforts and reminds us that He will give us the strength and the help we need by holding us through our journey by His righteous right hand.

This verse has great personal meaning as it is one that my dad recited through many detours and challenges in his life. It comforts me with the reassurance of God's presence. In spite of detours that bring dismay, loneliness, loss, and fear, I know God is there holding me. I love this image of being held and guided by my Lord. I may not know where the next turn is in the detour I am traveling, but I know that in my weakness and fear, He will be there to strengthen and hold me.

Depending on God's wisdom and His strength helps me recognize the gifts that He gives along the way. There are gifts, like the full moon we experienced, we receive even when we are traveling challenging detours. Sometimes, we do not appreciate those gifts until we get back to the familiar path. It is by looking backwards that we are able to recognize His unfailing grace.

What detour are you traveling today? No matter what put you on your unfamiliar path, *Fear not, do not be dismayed, the Lord is with you, He will strengthen you and help you by holding you in His righteous right hand.* —Isaiah 41:10. ♥

Devotions for the Distracted Heart

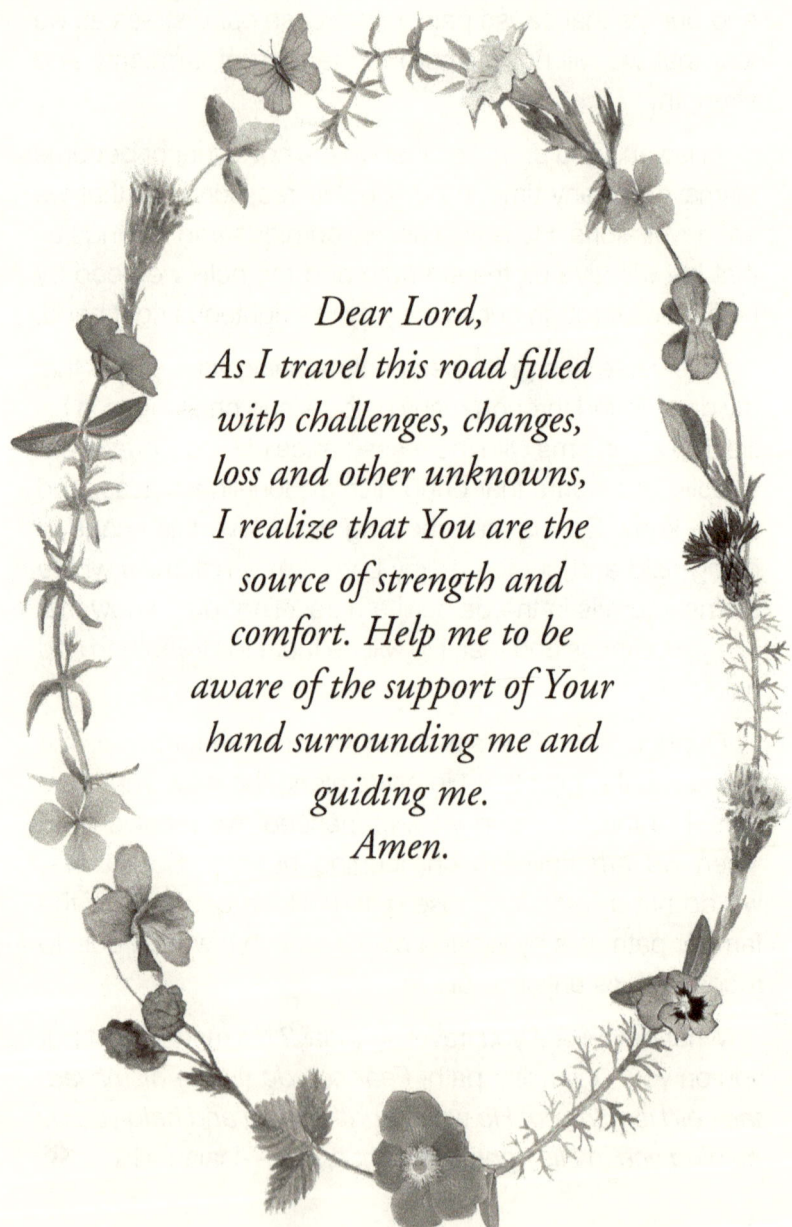

*Dear Lord,
As I travel this road filled with challenges, changes, loss and other unknowns, I realize that You are the source of strength and comfort. Help me to be aware of the support of Your hand surrounding me and guiding me.
Amen.*

Distraction of Doubt

> *Immediately Jesus reached out his hand and caught him. "You of little faith," he said, "why did you doubt?"*
> —Matthew 14:31

*H*ave you ever been in a situation where you had to step out of your comfort zone? During those times, did you feel a lack of confidence or unequipped to complete the assigned tasks? Think about a time that you were asked to take on a new endeavor, make a presentation, plan an event, teach a class, or accept some other responsibility.

Did you face it with confidence? Were you excited to "step out of the boat?" Or did you second guess yourself and ask:

Why me?

What do I have to offer?

Who wants to listen to me?

Why would they trust me?

Why didn't they ask her because she would do it so much better?

Or worse yet, *If they really knew me, they would never have asked me to do this!*

Devotions for the Distracted Heart

Doubt's internal messages can control, haunt, limit, and rob us of the confidence to accomplish a goal. It is a thorn that slivers into our spirits and festers into a wound that if untreated, could leave a scar for life. It may come from a voice in our past telling us we would never measure up. It may come from the comparisons of society that tell us we are too impatient, disorganized, young or old, heavy or thin, lazy, shy or outgoing, injured, too _____. *You fill in the blank.*

If we listen to these voices instead of God they will distract us from the gifts and abilities with which we are equipped and limit our own potential. Would we ever allow a child in our care to question his or her worth and abilities in the same way? Then why would we allow ourselves to fall into the trap of unworthiness and doubt?

I have to be honest with you. I experience times of doubt. Like Peter, when I am put into a situation of stepping out of the boat, I am not sure if I have the confidence or feel equipped to accomplish the task that's before me. My friends and family tell me that I have the abilities, but when preparing to speak, sing, perform, or even write these devotions, I am very vulnerable to those voices inside that say:

Who do you think you are?

What makes you think you have something worthwhile to share?

Why would others want to listen to you?

My stomach can become tied in knots, my legs shaky, or my insides feel like mush. Just as Peter doubted the ability

Distraction of Doubt

to walk on water with Christ, right there in front of him, I can doubt my God given abilities. Yet, when Peter kept his eyes on Christ, he remained on top of the water. When he looked away from Christ and doubted, he began to sink. I need to remember every day that doubt is not from God, and will limit what He can do through me. It is only by girding myself daily with the reassurance of God's word, and keeping my eyes on Him that I have the confidence to accomplish the tasks I am required to do. *I can do all things through Christ who gives me strength,* Philippians 4:13.

Do you believe that Christ has created you with gifts and equipped you with the abilities to do His will in whatever environment He has placed you? Do you feel God calling you into a new direction? Guard your mind and spirit from the voices of the world that want to distract you with doubt and fill you with lies of unworthiness. You are worthy. Step out of the boat, keep your eyes on Him, listen to His voice, and take His hand. Jesus will not let you sink!

*Dear Lord, Forgive me when I spend my time doubting the gifts and abilities You have entrusted to me. Help me to see myself as You do and ignore the doubts the world screams into my ear.
I want to hear Your voice, focus on Your eyes, and step out of my boat. Amen*

Distraction of Dislocation

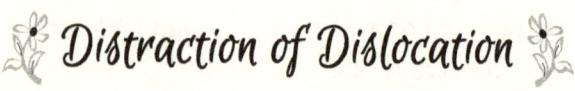

> *Have I not commanded you? Be strong and courageous. Do not be afraid; do not be discouraged, for the Lord your God will be with you wherever you go.*
> —Joshua 1:9

After living in Maryland for 40 years, 32 in the same house, preparing to move seemed overwhelming to say the least. A thousand questions filled my mind and billowed up like storm clouds threatening my sleep, decisions, security. There were decades of memories and accumulations to sort through. What should I keep? What should I throw away? What would my new life be like? How will I say good-bye to friends? What about my ministry? What have I done?

My husband and I had decided to relocate to Colorado to be close to our family. Our grown children and others had left Maryland and now we found ourselves separated by thousands of miles. As we researched the options, God seemed to be opening the door and paving the way for this cross-country move that felt foreign, frightening, and more like dislocation than relocation.

"Be strong and courageous. Do not be afraid; do not be discouraged, for the Lord your God will be with you

The Distraction of Dislocation

wherever you go," Joshua 1:9. The words jumped out of my devotion and eventually were given to us on a plaque signed by many friends at our Maryland church. Even while out on a walk, I questioned God about this move, I heard Him saying "What makes you think I have not prepared a place for you in Colorado?" Wow! Where was my trust? For years I had told myself and others to *trust in God with all your heart... or God has plans for you, plans to prosper you, not to harm you... Where was my trust in His faithfulness, His plans now?*

As I spent more time focusing on that trust, I began to discover the gifts of this new season ahead while allowing myself appropriate time to grieve what I was leaving behind. Many times my husband and I talked about the importance of gratitude. As I took time to savor the moments in Maryland, I focused more on the blessings by which I was surrounded rather than the losses I was experiencing.

There were even benefits in the downsizing process. Sorting through the "things" was a huge task, but not impossible. The goal was to keep the essentials and the treasures that provided a sense of heritage and home. With discipline and a bit of ruthlessness, I was able to dispose of more than 50% of our collected belongings.

Leaving friends was the biggest hurdle to grieve. We had known some of them for 40 years! They were more like family than just friends. Memories of raising kids and supporting each other through the ups and downs of life filled the legacy scrapbooks we shared. I discovered something very special in this process. Rather than look at this move like a dislocation or amputation from those relationships, God revealed a beautiful garden to me filled with mature oaks and tulip trees with deep roots that held fast during storms and verdant canopies that provided shade on bright sunny days. Beneath these beautiful trees, a cobblestone path meandered alongside hydrangeas, fragrant peonies, star gazer lilies, and colorful wildflowers.

As I asked God what this meant, He spoke again in a loving voice saying, "Some friends are brought into your lives for a season and some for a lifetime. The oak trees and tulip trees represent those friends of 20-40 years or more. The roots of your friendship are deep and have withstood the trials of storms and celebrated the joys of life. They will be here for you through every season, never impacted by distance or time. The lilies and wildflowers represent many assorted friends throughout the years, including those you will meet in your new home. They bring beauty, new growth, and support to your life. Some are there for a specific season and others will grow into the flowering bushes that will return each season healthy and strong."

Has the process of relocation been difficult? Of course, and just like a dislocated shoulder, there were times of challenge, tears, grief, healing, as well as joy. With each step, I received revelation from God and could hear His voice saying *"Be strong and courageous. Do not be afraid; do not be discouraged, for I the Lord your God will be with you wherever you go."*

Have you ever gone through a time when you felt dislocated, ripped out by your roots? It might be a change in your family or job, a heart-breaking loss, or a relocation. No matter what your situation, the process can be grueling

The Distraction of Dislocation

with many potholes and challenges along the way. But trusting in God's faithfulness can help you see His blessings in the midst of the mess. *Be strong and courageous. Do not be afraid; do not be discouraged, for the Lord your God will be with you wherever you go.* ♥

Dear Lord, You see the future, but I am surrounded by the challenges of the present. Forgive me when I fall into the traps of fear and frustration. Thank You for the relationships and friends You surround me with to help me navigate these difficult times. You are the source of strength and courage. Your faithfulness is always there to pull me out of the miry mess. Help me to focus on You and take Your hand. Amen